Observing Intelligence in Young Children

EIGHT CASE STUDIES

Observing Intelligence in Young Children

EIGHT CASE STUDIES

JEAN V. CAREW

Harvard Graduate School of Education

with

ITTY CHAN and **CHRISTINE HALFAR**

Harvard Graduate School of Education

Prentice-Hall, Inc. Englewood Cliffs, New Jersey

Library of Congress Cataloging in Publication Data

CAREW, JEAN V. (date)
  Observing intelligence in young children.

  1. Intellect—Case studies. 2. Child psychology—Case studies. I. Chan, Itty. (date), joint
author. II. Halfar, Christine. (date), joint
author. III. Title.
BF431.C269   155.4'13   75-22378
ISBN 0-13-628990-8
ISBN 0-13-628982-7 pbk.

Printed in the United States of America

10 9 8 7 6 5 4 3 2 1

The first names of all children and family initials
used in this book are fictitious and the accompanying
photographs are of parents and children who were not
participants in the research.

Photographs by Peter Gardner.
Illustrations by Kitty Riley Clark,
from *Experience and Environment: Major Influences*
on the Development of the Young Child, Vol. I,
by White,Watts et al. (Englewood Cliffs, N.J.: Prentice-Hall, Inc., 1973)

PRENTICE-HALL INTERNATIONAL, INC., London
PRENTICE-HALL OF AUSTRALIA, PTY. LTD., Sydney
PRENTICE-HALL OF CANADA, LTD., Toronto
PRENTICE-HALL OF INDIA PRIVATE LIMITED, New Delhi
PRENTICE-HALL OF JAPAN, INC., Tokyo
PRENTICE-HALL OF SOUTHEAST ASIA (PTE.) LTD., Singapore

To forty-eight families

and

to Antonia

who could not understand how observing children could be "work"

Contents

Foreword

The inspiration for writing this book was the remark of a friend, an excellent college teacher, who told me how difficult it sometimes was to make her course on early childhood development interesting because of the lack of case study material to give a concrete foundation to theory. Piaget's observations, though brilliant, were over-worked and over-quoted. Students quickly got tired of reading the same studies in textbook after textbook about Jacqueline and Laurent. The leading contender, Church's *Three Babies,* though useful, spoke like Piaget's observations to the experiences of upper-middle-class children of highly educated and articulate parents. The behavior of these *parents* toward their children was not observed any more than the behavior of Piaget himself as a *father.* Other case materials, like the earlier baby biographies, were too antiquated, still others too clinical or specialized in their themes. Popular books on child-rearing, on the other hand, were too imprecise and speculative. Needed was a book that described in detail the everyday experiences of a wide spectrum of "ordinary" children and that also showed how these experiences came about and what might be their effects on the children's development.

As I talked with my friend I realized that the research study my colleagues and I had just completed could provide precisely the type of information that she and her students were seeking. In this study we had observed the day-in, day-out experiences of forty-eight children—twenty-eight from age one to three and twenty from age two to three—in the normal, everyday environments of their homes and neighborhoods. These children came from the large variety of social class and ethnic back-

grounds represented in the Greater Boston area. More important, however, was that we had observed each child over a fairly long period of
time in a systematic fashion and had coded, quantified, and analyzed
these observations in terms of a conceptual framework designed to reveal
relationships between the child's everyday experiences, his environment,
and his intellectual development. The findings of this research would, we
hoped, be published in scholarly journals. But we were well aware that
few students would read these articles and even fewer parents and
teachers charged with the real responsibility of caring for young children.
Why not then a book that would be a qualitative rendition of our quantitative findings? Why not a set of case studies that would have a solid,
scientific basis in reflecting the methods and quantitative findings of our
research, yet be interesting and helpful in their own right?

The purpose was valuable, the means at hand, the audience dear
to us, and so this book was born. It is a book meant for students, teachers,
and parents interested in observing and interpreting the behavior of
young children. We hope it will stimulate not only scientific inquiry but
also increased interest and delight in the growth of young children and
commitment to action to enrich their lives. For in our own work and
living we find that the first has little enduring value in the absence of
the others.

JEAN V. CAREW

Acknowledgements

We wish to extend our gratitude first of all to the forty-eight families without whom this research simply would not exist. We were delighted with the cooperation, encouragement, and enthusiasm they showed towards our project, and with their friendliness, good humor, tolerance, and hospitality. We drank many good cups of coffee in their homes and would have liked to have known them much better than the rigid confines of scientific protocol allowed. These forty-eight families deserve the greatest credit for whatever interest in and benefit to children this research may inspire. We give thanks also to the families of the children photographed in this book who so charmingly spoke the language of behavior.

We wish also to thank others who have helped us in this project: Josefa Rosenberger, Connie Clemmens, and Anna DiPietrantonio, who typed and edited the manuscript; Tom Cerva and Anthony Bryk, who executed the statistical analyses in the research; Nancy Apfel and Geraldine Kearse Brookins, who were part of our team of observers; Kitty Clark, Bernice Shapiro, Ingrid Stocking and Marjorie Rekant, who were "the game ladies"; Peter Gardner, who made dozens of beautiful photographs; and Kitty Clark, who drew the cartoon figures. Thanks is also due to our co-workers on the Pre-School Project, with whom we collaborated on parts of the research and especially to Dr. Robert LaCrosse, whose work on environmental variables was helpful in the development of our understanding of mother-child interaction.

Great appreciation is also due to those who sponsored the research: the Office of Economic Opportunity, Head Start Division, and the Carnegie Corporation of New York. Particular people at these institutions gave us encouragement and help beyond the call of duty: Edith Grotberg and Mary Robinson at OEO, and Barbara Finberg at Carnegie. In addition, we received much needed help in locating the subjects of our study from personnel at various schools in the Boston area. Special thanks must go to Miriam Fiedler of the Maternal Infant Health Project and to B. Steinberg, who came to our rescue at a critical point in our recruitment efforts.

Very special thanks go to friends who reviewed parts of the manuscript and helped with timely criticism and encouragement: Marie Peters, Beatrice Whiting, Sara Lightfoot, Ragaa Mazen, and Chester Pierce.

Antonia Carew Watts, now six years old, was a special inspiration, although she never read a word of the book. We can only hope that when she learns to read "grown-up" books she will find this one worth reading.

AUTHORSHIP

Jean Carew wrote Chapters 1 and 4-8 of this work. Itty Chan wrote Chapter 2, and Jean Carew and Christine Halfar wrote Chapter 3. The author of each chapter takes primary responsibility for its content but all three of us shared to some extent in the preparation of every chapter in that we were all directly involved in collecting the research data, in selecting excerpts to illustrate the themes and case studies, and in discussing questions of interpretation.

Observing Intelligence in Young Children

EIGHT CASE STUDIES

Introduction

Studying the Child
in His Natural Environment

As early as the age of two or three striking differences in the intellectual development of children can be observed. Why and how do these differences come about? Do the experiences and environments that children encounter early in their lives have a significant effect on their development? The answers to these questions have eluded psychologists and practitioners for a long time for two reasons: we lack information as to what the everyday experiences of young children actually do consist of, and we lack a comprehensive framework for interpreting the meaning of these experiences for the child's development.

In this book we take a first step toward filling both these needs. Its purpose is to describe the everyday experiences and environments of eight one-year-old children whom we observed for two years in a rather unusual type of research study. Instead of bringing our child-subjects into a laboratory and asking them to perform tasks *we* deemed important, we went to their own homes and neighborhoods and observed month after month the ordinary experiences that they had with the familiar people, places, and things in their lives. Of each experience that we observed we asked the questions: what relevance and value did the particular experience have for the child's intellectual or social development? What was the child likely to be learning from it? What role did other people play in bringing it about, enhancing it, or restricting it?

We had two main purposes in gathering this type of information. The first was to describe in concrete detail the ordinary experiences of a broad cross section of children during a developmentally fundamental phase of their lives—the period from age one to three. The second was to compare the experiences of two contrasting groups of children: those who over the course of these two years developed very well intellectually and those who fared less well. In our research we paid particular attention to the role played by the child's main caregiver (usually his mother) in encouraging *intellectually valuable* experiences for her child. Specifically, we wanted to know: did the well-developed child have more frequent intellectually valuable encounters with his caregiver? Was she more likely to help bring about such experiences for her child even if she did not directly take part in them? Was she less likely to refrain from curtailing such experiences even when they seemed trivial, inconvenient or messy?

These are some of the specific questions that we shall try to answer in this book. We shall start by describing briefly the research on which our case studies are based in order to give the reader an idea of our methods of observation and interpretation and our major findings. We shall not go into much technical detail here. Our aim is simply to sketch the framework by which we judged the developmental value of the experiences these children had. This framework for interpreting experiences may, of course, be insufficient or incorrect. Recognizing this, our approach through this book is to describe verbatim many of the actual observations that we made on our subjects, leaving the reader free to arrive at his own interpretation of their developmental significance for the child. Our concern is not so much to determine which interpretation is right or wrong, but rather to show that some systematic framework for judging the value of ordinary childhood experiences must be constructed if we are to understand or influence development in young children.

The importance of this first step becomes apparent when we describe the wealth of varied experiences that young children have in their early years at home and compare the experiences of children who develop well intellectually versus those who develop less well. We do this in several ways. In chapter 2, "The Language of Behavior," we draw on observations from many children in the study to illustrate the typical experiences of the one- and two-year-old and the developmental value we attach to these experiences. The subject of this chapter is the child in action. Its main themes are that the child's day-to-day experience *is* the material that builds his intelligence and personality and that its developmental significance is conveyed in a language that another person can learn to decode through observation.

In the next chapter, "The Influence of People," our focus shifts from the child acting on a more or less passive environment to the child *interacting* with people. The theme here is the various roles which other actors—mother, father, brothers, sisters, friends—play in the child's experiences and the effects that their behavior may have on his development. This topic is especially important because our research shows that a critical ingredient in the basic mortar of childhood experience is the quality of the child's interaction with other human beings. The child who is exceptionally well-developed intellectually by age three is surrounded by people who help to bring about *intellectually valuable* experiences for him and who actively share these experiences with him; the child who develops less well has far fewer intellectually rich encounters with people in his life. Thus, the quality of interaction with other people is a key feature that distinguishes the experiences of the intellectually well-developing from the less well-developing child.

The remainder of this book is devoted to case studies of eight individual children who were subjects of our research. As in the preceding chapters, these case histories stay close to the actual observations of children's experiences that we recorded, but instead of discussing separate aspects of experience and environment illustrated by our observations on many different children as in chapters two and three, our purpose here is to describe more fully the experiences of individual children from age one to three, focussing on the role played by their mothers in their development.

The case studies are selected to elucidate issues of long standing interest to those concerned with the development of children. In the first pair of case studies (chapter 4) we analyze the experiences of two working-class children and focus on critical factors that seem to relate to their divergent intellectual development. In the second pair of studies (chapter 5) we question whether there is a formula that caregivers must follow in order to rear a well-developed child, and we point to the range of child-rearing styles that are compatible with excellent development outcomes. In the third (chapter 6) we address the question of social class differences in child-rearing values as they affect the intellectual and social development of one upper-middle-class girl and one working-class girl. In the fourth pair of case studies (given separately in chapters 7 and 8) we describe two cases of *extreme* environments—environments that, by almost any reasonable standard, would be considered deleterious to a child's development. In the first of these cases we describe a mother who, having severe psychological problems of her own, creates a highly stressful environment for her daughter, that seems to distort her development significantly. In the second we describe a child whose apparently autistic behavior would make it difficult for any ordinary mother to fashion an appropriate environment for him. Caught in the trap of his emotional disturbance he and his mother present extreme environments for each other that neither seems able to adapt to or to change.

In constructing the stories of these eight children our purpose is not to convince the reader of the correctness of our interpretations but rather to demonstrate what *can* be learned about the development of particular children by careful observation of their behavior over a span of time. For, this throughout is the message of this book. That the behavior of children is exciting to watch. That anyone interested in children can learn to observe and interpret their behavior. And that careful observation and interpretation makes both the study of children and the task of child-rearing more delightful, more challenging, and more effective.

1

A Natural Experiment

The term *natural experiment* captures three important aspects of the research study on which this book is based.* It is an apt description because it connotes first that we studied children in the natural milieu of their homes and neighborhoods rather than in an artificial laboratory setting. Second, we were interested in the role played in their intellectual and social development by their normal, everyday, encounters with people, places and things rather than in the effects of extraordinary traumatic events or special experiences contrived by social scientists. And third, we selected our subjects and organized our data so as to point up a contrast between two groups, much as if we were running a controlled experiment. One of these groups consisted of children who in the course of the study developed very well intellectually by the age of three; the other consisted of children who developed less well. Our purpose in selecting and comparing these two groups was to arrive at answers to some simple but fundamental questions. In what way did the experiences of these children differ prior to age three? Was the part played by their environments in their experiences demonstrably different? How were dis-

*The methods and findings of the research are described preliminary form in Burton White, Jean Carew Watts, Itty Chan Barnett, Barbara Kaban, and Bernice Shapiro, *Environment and Experience: Major Influences on the Development of the Young Child* (Englewood Cliffs, N.J.: Prentice-Hall, 1973). A fuller description may be found in Jean V. Carew, Itty Chan, and Christine Halfar, in "Observed intellectual competence and tested intelligence: their roots in the young child's transactions with his environment." Paper presented at the Biennial Meeting of the Society for Research in Child Development, Denver, Colorado, 1975.

similarities in their environments and experiences related to their divergent
intellectual development?

WHO, WHEN, AND WHERE WE OBSERVED

The subjects of the study were forty-six white and two black children
from a variety of social class and cultural backgrounds who were either
one or two years old when we started observing them. We observed each
child in his own home or neighborhood for about one hour on five separate
occasions between the ages of two or more of the following periods:
12-15, 18-21, 24-27 and 30-33 months. We visited the home at various
times of day between 9 a.m. and 5 p.m., weekdays, asking the mother or
caregiver to follow her normal routine while we were there and to let
her child do the same. Each observation consisted of a forty-minute tape-
recorded description of the child's activities and of the human and physical environment insofar as it played a role in these activities.

Despite some practical and technical constraints on our observations,
the range of people, places, things and activities that we observed was
quite extraordinary. We saw children interacting with relatives, neighbors,
friends and strangers. We followed them in living rooms, basements,
playgrounds, shopping centers and museums. We observed them in an
astonishing array of activities—from play with dolls and trucks, to exploration of knives and electrical outlets, to the ecstasy of sprinkler showers,
mud baths and genital stimulation. No activity was too trivial or intimate
for our observing eyes. Each was judged for its relevance and value to
the child's intellectual and social development.

WHY DID WE OBSERVE?

The observer's principal task as she scrambled after her child-subject was
to describe accurately and systematically the child's experiences in terms
of their importance to his intellectual and social development. What toys
did he play with? How did he play with them? What skills did he seem
to be trying to master? How did he approach other people? Why? The
observer's first visit to the child's home was followed by nineteen others
spaced over two of the most formative years of his life—from age one to
three. The information gathered from these twenty visits was then together to form a rich profile of his behavior revealing progressive changes
in his intellectual and social experiences as he matured.

The observer's second aim in visiting the home was to describe how
people who came into contact with the child—especially his mother—

influenced his experiences. How much time did they spend playing with him, talking, teaching, scolding, praising him? When they played together what form did the play take? What objects were used? What topics were touched on? What style was employed? The observer's final aim was to map the relationships between the child's experiences, his environment, and his intellectual development. The latter was charted by means of periodic tests and evaluations made from the time the child was one to when he turned three.

JUDGING THE INTELLECTUAL VALUE
OF THE CHILD'S EXPERIENCE

Our basic observational records contain a vast amount of information on the experiences of our subject children. In order to reduce the data to manageable proportions and answer the basic research questions, we begin by coding the data in terms of certain categories. The first set of categories deals with the child's moment-to-moment experiences or activities considered primarily in terms of their relevance and value to his intellectual development.

We believe that an observer can be trained to judge the intellectual value of an experience for a child on the basis of the content and style of the child's own behavior and/or of an environmental input that may be part of the experience. In our research, we consider intellectually valuable those experiences that seem to provide an opportunity for the child to learn the following four types of skills. The first type involves experiences that enable the child to learn new *words, symbols* or *information.* In these experiences the child is typically engaged in labeling objects, counting, reciting nursery rhymes or children's songs, looking at books, recalling past events, or stating novel facts about the physical or social environment; or else he is attentive to another person, live or on television, doing one of these things. The second type of experiences provides an opportunity for the child to master *perceptual, spatial* and *fine motor skills.* The child is usually engaged in tasks of fitting, stacking, building, or matching, distinguishing and ordering objects by size, shape, color or position; or else he is observing someone else doing one of these things. The third type of experiences gives the child the opportunity to learn basic *reasoning skills,* such as differentiating means from ends and cause from effect, and to learn about the *basic physical laws and regularities* underlying such concepts as object permanence, volume, gravity, momentum, buoyancy, trajectory, equilibrium, and reflection. In these instances the child is engaged in little "scientific" experiments with objects that sail or sink, things that plummet or float gently to the ground, containers that hold

**ACTIVITIES OF ONE-
AND TWO-YEAR OLDS**

Learning to walk

Making a headstand

Trying out a shovel

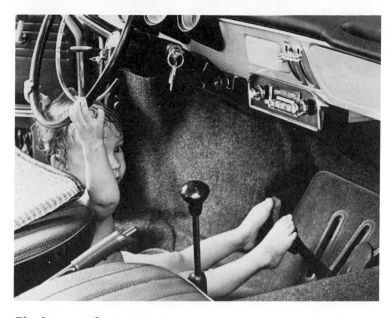

Checking out the car

At the beach

more or less liquid, objects that cast shadows or reflections, and mechanisms that work in interesting ways. The child's focus seems to be on understanding basic physical regularities and relationships through varying his own actions on appropriate objects or noticing these phenomena serendipitously as they occur. The fourth category of intellectually valuable experiences provides the child with the opportunity to learn *expressive or artistic skills*. Typically he is involved in make-believe, in role-play, in making such representational products as a monster painting or a sand castle, or in such expressive activities as playing a musical instrument or trying to whistle or carry a tune; or else he is attentive to another person doing one of these things. We say "or else he is attentive to another person . . ." because it must be stressed that in each case the intellectually valuable content of the experiences may come either from the child himself *or* from another human, live or on television, whose behavior the child observes.

We turn now to those characteristics of the child's behavior that, according to the observer, show that the child is actively creating an intellectually valuable experience for himself, rather than passively receiving one from his environment. The child between ages one and three is mostly an *active* child. What he is thinking about and how he is thinking about it are likely to be directly reflected in the way he behaves. The child of this age certainly does learn from observing and listening passively, but his most frequent means of learning is *active* interchange with his environment. This does not mean that all experiences in which a child is active are automatically intellectually valuable for him. A child may run helter-skelter from room to room or flit about from object to object or engage in a variety of routine behaviors, and it would be absurd to consider these activities as promoting his intellectual development. Other criteria than mere "activity" need to be introduced.

These criteria have to do with the involved, purposeful, organized, constructive and/or creative nature of the behavior of the child who is creating an intellectually valuable experience for himself. Such a child is highly involved in what he is doing and seems to be organizing his activity toward the mastery of some skill or idea. For example, he may systematically explore or manipulate an object as if trying to understand its qualities (as when he mouths, bangs, and shakes a block); he may vary his actions on the object as if to test out their effects (as when he pours sand into a container from different heights and angles); he may execute a series of steps culminating in some product (as when he makes a snake from playdough); he may struggle to master a skill (as when he learns to cut with scissors); he may attach new labels to objects or make distinctions among classes ("this cookie is good; this cookie is 'gooder'"); or he may act out a story in make-believe (as when he pretends to cook and feed his dog "a nice, warm dinner"). In judging the intellectual value of the child's behavior the observer pays attention to *process* rather than *product*. Wrong answers achieved after a struggle are as indicative of intellectual development as are right ones; clumsy execution is as acceptable as smooth. The qualities of involvement, struggle, organization, purposefulness and creativity are the principal cues on which the observer bases her judgment that certain types of child behavior are themselves of *high* intellectual value to the child. Activity that is considered to be of *less* intellectual value tends to have a routine, unstructured, random, or empty quality, as when the child carries out a well-learned habit, or makes run-of-the-mill comments, or engages in simple, unorganized exploration, or simply seems to be doing or looking at nothing in particular.

Finally, it must be emphasized that in making the judgment that an experience is intellectually valuable the observer has to go far beyond the use of educational materials or the receiving of lessons in the manner of the classroom. If these were the only criteria for considering an experience intellectually stimulating there would be little to record, because the everyday experiences of children at home are seldom so didactic. The observer's task is far more subtle. It is to see the intellectual value of informal events—such as making cookies or getting dressed—that mother or child transforms into learning situations. Any situation, no matter how mundane, can become an intellectually profitable experience for the child depending on what is put into it.

A picture, they say, is worth a thousand words. So we shall sum up the distinctions we make between experiences of greater and less intellectual value by means of an illustration that shows how the same situation— "child is being diapered"— can give rise to experiences judged to be more or less intellectually stimulating for the child.In the first picture of *Figure 1* mother changes the diaper and the child simply gazes about. There is little evidence that any intellectual learning is going on. In the second picture the child uses the moment for a new kind of experience, as he explores the powder box while his mother looks on. This situation would be considered as moderately likely to promote learning. In the last two pictures the mundane and typically nonintellectual situation of being changed has become the setting for two experiences judged to be of high intellectual value for a young child. In the third picture the child is learning about the process of putting on powder. In the fourth picture the child is practicing another high level skill for toddlers, that of lacing shoes. The point of this illustration is to show that in coding experiences our decision is not determined by the kind of material or the overall context of the activity; but rather it reflects a judgment of what the child is likely to be learning from his own behavior and that of others, no matter how banal the setting.

Figure 1.   Distinction among highly, moderately, and nonintellectual activities.

EVALUATING THE HUMAN ENVIRONMENT

So far we have described how the child's own behavior in an experience is evaluated in our coding system. Let us turn now to the role that the human environment plays in those experiences. We start by assuming that interpersonal interactions help to promote or hinder a child's development. That is, they can provide important opportunities for learning which affect the child's intelligence and personality. One can conceive of many alternative evaluations of an interactor's role. The system we have chosen to use in our research organizes the types of behavior people normally use with young children into four major categories. These are labelled *active participation, facilitation, observation* and *restriction.*

Active participation occurs when the interactor plays an integral part in the child's experience, taking the role of an entertainer, playmate, teacher, helper, or conversant. Facilitation occurs when the interactor helps the child to realize the experience for himself—for example, by suggesting the activity, granting permission, providing desired materials or praising and encouraging the child. Observation is involved when the interactor merely listens to the child or observes him. Finally, restriction means that the interactor attempts to prevent or inhibit the child's experience. The basic underlying idea in this system is that another person can help intellectually valuable experiences to happen or not happen for a child, and can make them more likely or less likely to recur in the future.

Once again these distinctions seem best expressed by pictures rather than words. The first set of pictures *(Figure 2)* shows several types of participation. Here "Creative Cathy" is producing a work of art and her mother shares in this noble experience by actively joining in, by teaching her a trick or two, and by chatting enthusiastically about her amazing feat. The second set of pictures *(Figure 3)* shows several types of restriction. "Eager Eddie" is running a scientific experiment on flotation which doesn't quite win his father's approval. His father restricts him by bodily removal, by a sharp scolding, then finally by that most effective maneuver of all—distraction to an even more exciting enterprise. The third group of pictures *(Figure 4)* sums up the distinctions made among three of the four major categories of techniques: observation, restriction and participation. First, Mother merely observes "Precocious Pat" reading *Playboy*. Next she restricts her, apparently administering a torrential scolding. Third (highly improbable though it is) she gets involved in the activity, looking at the pictures with her daughter and explaining about the parts of the body and the curious use of bunny-rabbits in the illustrations!

One should note a certain difference in the participatory behavior of the mother in Figure 2 and Figure 4(c). In Figure 2 both Cathy and her mother are actively involved in producing the pictures, and the experience is made intellectually valuable for Cathy because of her own behavior as well as that of her mother. In contrast, in Figure 4(c) Pat's behavior is limited to looking and listening to her mother's explanation of body parts and bunnies, and it is primarily the mother who provides the intellectual content of the child's experience. In situations like this in which the child is passive but attentive to an environmental input—whether he is listening to his mother's teachings, or watching Sesame Street, or observing his sister construct a model airplane—it is primarily the content and style of the environmental input rather than that of the child's own behavior that determine the observer's judgment of the intellectual value of the child's experience.

MAJOR FINDINGS OF THE RESEARCH

Now that we have given the reader some idea of what an intellectually valuable experience might consist of and how it might come about from the child's own active behavior and/or from an environmental input, let us examine briefly the major findings of the research study from which the observations presented in this book are taken.*

*The study referred to is that of White, Watts et al. (1973) previously cited. The case studies of Matthew and Diana were developed from the expansion of that study by Carew, Chan and Halfar (1975), also cited previously.

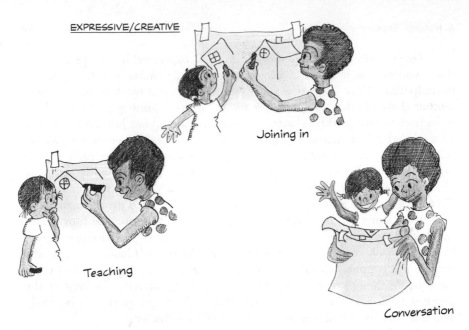

Joining in

Teaching

Conversation

Figure 2. Mother uses participatory techniques of teaching, joining in, and conversation in an expressive/creative activity.

CONCRETE REASONING

Prevention

Scolding

Distraction

Figure 3. Father uses restrictive techniques of prevention, scolding, and distraction in a concrete reasoning activity.

VERBAL/SYMBOLIC

Figure 4.   Mother uses techniques of observation, restriction, and participation in a verbal/symbolic activity.

As previously mentioned, the major purpose of our "natural experiment" was to compare the environments and experiences encountered by two groups of children in their everyday living from age one to three. One group consisted of children who, by the time they turned three, seemed to be very well developed intellectually while the other group was composed of children who at the same age seemed considerably less well developed. Each child's intellectual functioning was evaluated both in terms of his observed behavior in his home environment and in terms of his performance on such standardized tests as the Bayley Mental Scales of Infant Development, administered at age one and two, and the Stanford Binet given at age three. Though there were a few individual inconsistencies, on the whole these two types of assessment provided strikingly similar results. Thus at age three, the median Stanford Binet IQ for the group of intellectually well-developed children whom we observed from age one was 122, whereas for the group of intellectually less well developed children it was 86. Similarly, in our observations of them at home, the first group much more frequently behaved in ways that impressed observers as "intelligent" than the second group, the difference becoming more and more marked as the children grew older.

In what way were the experiences and environments that these two groups of children had had prior to age three related to the contrasting outcomes? The answer lies in understanding how intellectually valuable experiences come about for the young child in his everyday milieu. First, our findings show that the young child is to a considerable extent the originator and creator of his own intellectual experiences. If intellectual skills and ideas are learned, the child is often his own teacher. Through his own efforts he generates a variety of experiences for himself that simultaneously reflect and promote his intellectual development.

But second, and equally important, is the role played by the child's environment—especially his human environment. A key finding of the research study is that the people who come into regular contact with the well-developed child are much more likely to participate actively and directly in his intellectual experiences than is the case for the less well-developed child. Their participation in his intellectual experiences goes far beyond merely reacting to his behavior in an encouraging or supportive manner. It often includes their taking the initiative in *creating* an intellectual experience for the child by providing information, ideas, and know-how that, at the time, are somewhat beyond his capabilities. The other person's behavior serves to challenge the child, to present novel concepts, information and skills, and to expand, elaborate, or improve ideas and skills he is in the process of mastering. Just as the child learns from his own active, organized, constructive and creative behavior so he learns from similar behavior on the part of other people who engage in intellectually profitable activities with him.

These two simple truths—that the child learns both from what he does for himself and from what others do with him—have, in theory and practice, too often been put into false opposition with one another, as if they were mutually exclusive. The purpose of this book is to show in concrete detail just how both types of learning can be interwoven in the young child's everyday life and how both become the essence of his intellectual development.

2

The Language
of Behavior

The young child is a spontaneous and resourceful explorer of his environment. He is constantly trying out something, putting things together, practicing what he can do and studying the actions of others. He is active and inventive in constructing experiences for himself that will contribute to his development as a growing being. Such developmental experiences include both practical acquaintance with and deliberate observation of his environment.

Growing and learning are not something done to a child nor something a child does entirely by himself. The child makes contact with the world of people and things around him to learn about it and to construct his intelligence and personality from it. Simultaneously the world becomes an integrated part of the child's experiences, reflected in his intelligence, personality and memory. Experiencing is a continuous process of interaction, a process of *coming together* between the child and his human and physical environment. The child and his environment have a reciprocal relationship: in any given situation the child brings himself, his capabilities and all his previous experiences, while the environment—in human or material form—brings its stimulating and responsive qualities. Both the child and his environment interact to determine his development.

What is the child like at the end of his first year of life, and what makes his active construction of experience possible? Let us take a brief look. The average child at age one has the *physical maturity* that enables him to cruise, to crawl, to pull himself up, to reach up on tip-toe and to walk. This new ability to move about makes it possible for him to be present in a greater range of places and situations and consequently to construct a wider variety of experiences than before. He also shows better eye-hand coordination that enables him to grasp, poke, pinch, and manipulate objects in various ways, as well as to touch, hold, and wave to people. This growing capacity makes it possible for him to try out his actions upon things and people and to discover the effects of his actions.

The child at age one also has a better understanding of what is happening to him and around him. He has a better comprehension of adult language. When he hears his mother say, "Let's get your *bottle* and go *night-night*," he can expect to see food and to be put in his crib. Or when he tries to pull an electric cord at the plug outlet and hears a "no-no," he can expect his exploration to be stopped. Or when he hears, "Here comes Susan," he can expect his sister to appear at the door.

The child is also more keenly aware of the relationships between his actions and those of other people. When he offers his mother his half-eaten cookie, his mother smiles and says "thank you." When he tries to take a toy truck from his brother, his brother pushes him and grabs the toy truck back. When he sees a playmate go to kiss her mother and gets a hug in return, he goes to kiss his mother and gets a kiss back, too. Thus, the child has come to see the connections between his actions and the responses of others, and this increasing awareness guides him in his experiencing of events and situations.

The child at age one also has an increasing capability to express himself as a separate person. He has strong wishes and feelings of his own and expresses or communicates them by gestures, vocalizations, actions, and sometimes words. When he has enough supper, he may close his mouth and turn his head away to refuse more food. When he sees an ant, he may say "ah-ah" until he can bring his mother's attention to it. When he is angry, he may throw himself on the floor and cry. He actively brings people to him and alerts them to his own wishes, feelings, and needs, and finds out about their reactions in expressing himself. The child exercises his "power" upon his immediate environment and learns about the influence and impact he has on the world of people and things around him. In short, at the end of his first year of life, the child has become more perceptually aware of, more actively involved in, and more socially conscious of his environment. He is curious and resourceful in finding out all about it for himself.

To provide a picture of how young children construct developmental experiences, we shall use a number of excerpts taken verbatim from our observations of one- to three-year-old children. Of course, these records only illustrate the small portions of children's experiences that are observable and open to interpretation. Often it is difficult to know what a child's behavior really means for his development. For example, when a child watches a television program attentively, but without explicit reactions, how can we tell what the child absorbs and what specific connections he makes in his mind? Is the *Lucy Show* any less educational than *Sesame Street* for a one- to three-year-old? If we judge simply on the basis of the child's behavior, we cannot be sure of our answer. The following excerpts from our real-life observations, therefore, are limited to situations in which the observer is able to take cues from the child's behavior, thereby making reasonable interpretations about his experiences.

These excerpts and discussion of their meaning are organized according to two of the child's primary modes of experiencing the world on his own—namely, through actions and through observation and imitation. The young child's other major means of experiencing the environment—through interaction with people and through language—are discussed in chapter 3.

EXPERIENCING THE ENVIRONMENT THROUGH ACTIONS: ACTING ON THE WORLD TO CREATE NEW EXPERIENCES

The young child most often learns by *doing*. He acts upon everything that happens to interest him and is delighted at what he can do. He may *manipulate* something in order to discover what it is like (exploration); he may *practice* doing something (mastery); or he may *test* out what he can do to something (experimentation). We shall illustrate each of these approaches by excerpts from our observations, beginning at age one and continuing to the ripe old age of three.

Experiences of Exploration

By manipulating and investigating objects, children come to discover what things feel like, look like, sound like, taste like; they learn how the parts make up the whole, how components fit together, how mechanisms work. Their focus in experiences of exploration is on the qualities of objects themselves. They are, so to speak, ingesting or assimilating their physical environments. Here are several excerpts illustrating typical explorations of young children.

Tactual qualities. We start with Lisa, age twelve months. Lisa is fascinated by the feeling of a damp metal surface. It feels cold and slippery. But how does it sound? She finds out by banging a metal spoon first on the metal tray, then, for contrast, on a plastic surface.

> Lisa is sitting in a highchair as her mother feeds her baby food. Lisa slides her finger on the damp surface of the feeding tray which her mother has just wiped. Lisa starts to bang a spoon in her other hand on the metal tray. She

**EXPLORING HOW
A CAT FEELS**

EXPLORING THE LOOK AND TASTE OF SAND

eats and continues banging. Mother says, "That is a spoon." Lisa eats and bangs the spoon on the metal tray. She then bangs the spoon on the plastic bowl and listens to the different sound it produces. Lisa smiles and continues eating and banging alternately on the tray and bowl, chuckling with delight at the contrast in sounds.

Varying actions. Turn now to Danny, fourteen months and brimming with curiosity. The object Danny studies as he stands in his playpen is rather commonplace—a plastic string from a wind-up car. But Danny's exploration is thorough. He savors the feeling of the smooth, cool surface of the plastic line, he studies the elegant arc of its shape, and he investigates its pliancy by waving it carefully and deliberately in the air.

Danny holds a curved plastic line that has come off a wind-up car. Danny puts the line in his mouth and vocalizes, his saliva dripping down the line. Danny chews on the line, waves it, chews it, then waves the line again, turning his head and watching the line turn in the air (it makes an interesting, curving motion). He waves his arm and watches the line wiggle in midair. Danny drops the line over the playpen rail.

Animation. Now comes one of our favorite examples. It is about Nora, an eighteen-month-old girl who studies the family cat's tail and how it moves when she pulls it. So carried away is Nora by her discoveries that she imitates the rhythmic movement of the cat's tail with her hands as if miming the theme: What is it like to be a pussy-cat?

Nora crawls under the kitchen table and sits near the family cat. She pulls up the cat's tail and brushes her stomach with the tail. The cat meows and moves away. Nora hits the cat and says, "Don't." Nora again picks up the end of the cat's tail but the cat pulls away. Nora pulls again and the cat pulls away again, bristling up in annoyance. She watches intently as the cat's tail flicks back and forth. She laughs and moves her hand back and forth, almost in rhythm with the cat's tail. Nora clicks her tongue and calls "kitty, kitty," babbling to the cat. She strokes the cat and drinks from her bottle.

Mechanisms. How do the components of a machine fit together? What makes it work? These are two-year-old Linda's questions as she investigates the mysteries of a flashlight by taking it apart and trying to put it back together.

Linda picks up a flashlight from the living room couch. She unscrews the head and takes it apart. She looks inside where the light bulb is, then looks at the empty compartment where batteries are normally kept. Linda looks at the head then tries to screw it back on without success. Linda puts the wrong side of the head against the battery compartment and tries to screw it on. She looks at the lightbulb, takes it out, examines it, then fits it back on the head. Linda turns the head to the right side against the battery compartment

**EXPLORING HOW
THINGS WORK**

and tries to screw it on again, but fails again. She continues struggling with the flashlight.

A similar question challenges Neil. Thirty-four months old, Neil is helping his mother make cookie dough. This exciting occasion presents an opportunity for him to investigate still another marvelous mechanism—the flour sifter.

> Neil is helping Mother make cookie dough. Mother holds the flour sifter for Neil to squeeze the handle in order to sift the flour. Neil squeezes and listens intently to the sound made by the mechanism. He picks up the sifter and begins to explore it systematically. He squeezes the handle, turns it over, and looks intently at the mechanism underneath, as if studying how it works. He says to Mother, "I am going to shake it again."

Experiences of Mastery

By practicing specific motor skills the young child develops the skill itself and learns to apply it appropriately to suitable objects. He also learns about the characteristics of objects and about certain fundamental physical laws and concepts.

Fitting, stacking and building. A skill which young children love to practice is that involved in fitting one object into another, stacking objects one on top of the other, and using objects to construct a building. Younger children will devote extraordinary amounts of time and effort to fitting lids on pots and pans, placing plastic doughnuts on pegs, or putting blocks of different shapes into the corresponding holes of a shape box. Older children continue to be fascinated by the problem of the match, although they are more likely to use puzzles or construction toys in their drive for mastery.

The following excerpts illustrate the young child's interest in mastering fine motor skills and in understanding spatial relations.

We start with Becky, twelve months old, as she tries to fit a finger puppet into a container which is much too small to hold it. Although an adult can clearly see the impossibility of the task, Becky, with her infantile understanding of size-relations, is undeterred from attempting the impossible.

> Becky tries to fit a finger puppet into a miniscule plastic toy trunk. She manages to put the bottom part of it in, then tries to push the trunk toys down on it by force. The puppet is obviously too big for the toy trunk, and as soon as Becky lets go her hand, the puppet pops up again. Becky tries to squeeze the puppet down inside the trunk several times. She looks puzzled, then toddles away to join a ball game her sister is starting.

Turn now to Benjamin, eighteen months old, as he plays with a set of nesting cups at the kitchen table.

Benjamin takes off the lid of the largest cup, sets it down and places the cup to one side. He then does the same with the next two cups, stacking the lids and setting the cups in a row of three from smallest to largest. Ben now takes off the lids of the remaining three cups and stacks the lids on the previous three. He adds the remaining three cups to his row of three, arranging them in ascending order from smallest to largest. Ben gets down from the kitchen table, runs to his mother and returns at full speed, his mother following him.

He now turns the largest cup of the row upside down. Mother observes and questions: "What are you making, Ben?" Ben replies: "Tower," and begins stacking the cups, the largest one at the bottom, and the others in descending order of size.

Ben asks his mother: "Where is another cup?" Mother says: "I don't know what you mean." Ben points to the very top of his tower: "To put in here." Mother says: "Oh, another cup to put on that one? There aren't anymore, Ben. That's all they made. If there was another one, it would be so small you might lose it." Ben touches the tower. Mother says: "It is very nice. Do you want to put the cover on top?" Ben carefully puts the smallest lid on top of the smallest cup on the very top of the tower as Mother watches.

Cutting, tying and drawing. The basic skill involved in fitting, stacking and building is not dissimilar to that of cutting, tying and drawing, although the latter group usually requires more difficult coordination of two hands and the understanding of more complex spatial relationships. We are thus more likely to see older children undertaking these tasks, with the quality of concentration and drive to master the skill remaining the same. Consider Tom, thirty-one months old and interested in learning how to handle a knife.

Tom cuts a carrot stick with the dull side of his knife and has a hard time cutting through it. The carrot stick rolls to the side of his plate. Tom turns the knife, sharp side down, and tries to cut the carrot but it is too close to the edge of the plate and the knife cannot go down. Tom tries it with the dull side down. Mother notices and says, "Wait, turn it over, see?" and helps Tom turn the sharp side of his knife down on the carrot. Tom tries to cut again, but the edge of the plate is still in the way. Mother says, "Oh, the edge of the plate. Move it up here." She helps Tom move the carrot to the center of the plate, where he has enough room for his knife to cut down into the carrot. Tom continues cutting carrots while his mother watches, encouraging him from time to time.

We see similar intense concentration in Kate, thirty-three months old, as she tries to tie a knot on a box, a task which involves intertwining patterns, as well as sequential steps in two-hand coordination. Like Tom, Kate seems to enjoy the challenge and persists at her task for a long time, even though at the end it doesn't turn out exactly as she had planned.

SOLVING A JIGSAW PUZZLE

Kate runs to Mother calling, "I am going to help you." (Mother is tying a box with a piece of parcel post string.) Kate looks on as Mother puts the string around the box. Mother says, "You do this, I'll hold this." Mother puts her finger down on the string to hold it in place and asks Kate to tie a knot. Kate takes the end of the string and tries to make a knot as Mother looks on. She tries to put one end of the string under the other end without success. Mother says, "Try again." Kate tries again. Mother helps by lifting one end and says, "Want to put that under there?" Kate says, "Cut." Mother says, "Don't cut it yet until you tie it." Kate tries again but fails. Mother: "Put that under," and makes a loop for Kate. Kate follows instructions. Mother says, "Now you make another loop." Mother observes Kate make the loop. Mother: "Now pull them." Kate pulls one end. Mother (demonstrating with her hands): "Pull both strings, pull that one that way, and this one this way." Kate pulls hard but the knot comes apart. Mother says: "Oh, it didn't turn out to be a knot!" They both laugh at Kate's fiasco.

Sometimes a child may be so totally involved in the process of performing a given action (often in practicing a newly acquired skill) that he may not pay much attention to the object itself nor to the consequences of his actions. The skill may become an end in itself rather than a means to some goal. In the following account, thirty-month old Sandra becomes so absorbed in the task of shaking something out of a container that she forgets at one point to place the paprika-shaker down and later tries to "shake" a piece of green pepper onto the chicken while holding onto it. Sandra needs her mother's gentle guidance to see that there is a relationship between what she is doing and what she is doing it to.

Sandra is helping her mother make paprika chicken. Sandra shakes paprika from a shaker onto the chicken. The holes on the can are blocked and Sandra calls to Mother, "Won't work." Mother: "Won't work?" and picks the holes open for Sandra. Sandra looks at the top of the can: "Oh, dear, there's a hole." She resumes shaking more paprika on the chicken and says, "Now making more." Mother looks on and shows her where she should shake more by pointing. Sandra continues shaking for some time while Mother works beside her.

Sandra says to Mother: "It don't work." Mother says, "It doesn't work?" and unblocks the top again for Sandra. Sandra starts to shake again but forgets to turn the can upside down. She shakes and shakes and nothing comes out on the chicken. Sandra tells Mother, "It don't work." Mother looks and says, "It doesn't work? Why? Tell me why?" Sandra looks at the paprika can and, as if realizing what she was doing wrong, turns it upside down and shakes some paprika out (too much, apparently). Sandra says to Mother, "Look what happened." Mother tells her not to worry about the spill. Sandra says, "Get a better one." Mother: "Okay," and hands a jar of soy sauce to Sandra.

Sandra pours soy sauce on the chicken. Mother says, "That's good. Now you can put these all over the chicken," as she puts pieces of cut up green pepper near Sandra. Sandra picks up a pepper piece and shakes it above

the chicken as if it were the paprika can. Mother says, "You just drop those
on, they'll fall on the chicken." Sandra picks up some pepper pieces and
throws a few on the chicken in the pan. Mother says, "That's right." Sandra
puts more pepper pieces on and says, "More." Mother replies, "Yes, put
many on. I love peppers."

Experiences of Experimentation

From experiences of mastery we turn now to experiences of experimentation, in which the child's interest no longer lies in mastering a skill but
rather on trying out varying ways of acting on familiar objects to test what
effects his actions bring about. As in scientific experimentation, the child
is anticipating novel outcomes from his different combinations of objects
and actions. He is deliberately controlling his physical environment and
creating new experiences for himself. He is generating his own "wonderful
ideas" and reinventing the laws of nature. Here are some of the questions
which our one- and two-year-old scientists consider worth investigating.

Gravity and trajectory. Where will a thing fall? Will it land or fly?
At twelve months Dean is experimenting with the laws of gravity and
trajectory by throwing toys out of his playpen and watching them fall.

Dean sits in the playpen. His older sister comes in with an armful of toys
and puts them into the playpen. Dean picks up a spoon and a toy chicken.
He throws the chicken out of the playpen onto the living room floor and leans
forward to watch it fall. He mouths the spoon. He bends down to pick up a
small wooden doll and the toy chicken and throws them out onto the floor.
His mother sees this and says to him in a pleasant voice, "Uh!—Now, you
haven't got them." Dean looks at his mother and claps his hands. Mother
claps her hands back and calls, "Hey, Dean!"

Twelve months older than Dean, Mark's research topic is similar.
His materials are toy cars, a cushion for an incline and his own body to
test firsthand the sensations of rolling.

Mark pushes a seat cushion off the couch in the living room, so that it lands
on the floor and leans on the couch as an incline. Mark slides a toy car down
on the incline, then another, then another. He gets on the couch and slides
himself down on the cushion incline. He gets up and picks up all the cars and
repeats the game. Mark lines up two cars on the top of the incline and pushes
them down at the same time then slides the other cars down one by one.
Mark picks up the cars and slides them down again and then slides down
himself on his tummy.

Mark's experiment reminds us of Ted, who introduces an amusing
variation on Mark's theme in an experiment with trajectories.

Ted walks around in the living room, swinging a yo-yo. He whirls himself around in circles and watches the yo-yo swing and wrap itself around his body. Ted whirls around in the opposite direction, so that the yo-yo unwinds from him then wraps itself around him again from the opposite side. Ted repeats the game, whirling himself around in one direction then the other, so that the yo-yo winds around him then unwinds, winds around him from the other side then unwinds. He continues repeating the sequence for several minutes.

Floating bodies. Why do some things float and others sink? At thirteen months Brenda tries to answer this question scientifically. The topic of her experiment is the law of floating bodies; her materials are a glass of milk, some lumps of meat, and a couple of potato chips.

Brenda sips a glass of milk in her highchair. She pushes the glass away, sliding it along the table top. Suddenly she drops a piece of meat into the glass and it sinks. She startles slightly and then deliberately puts a potato chip in and it floats. She looks puzzled. Brenda puts her hand deep into the glass and seems to be searching for the piece of meat at the bottom. She lifts the glass toward her, peers into it then pushes it away. Brenda puts her hand in again and waves her fingers about in the milk several times as if trying to reach the meat.

Object permanence. Does a thing continue to exist when I cannot see it? Lucy, at twelve months, is intrigued by the phenomenon of object permanence. She is playing a game dear to generations of children—peek-a-boo. Her fascination with this game is in making the room and her mother vanish each time she covers her eyes and reappear each time she pulls off the cover. Lucy probably already understands that her mother is not doing a disappearing act but continues to exist even while she, Lucy, cannot see her. This realization is a short step toward understanding concepts of monumental significance to a child—such as that her mother continues to exist even when she, Lucy, has been put to bed; or that her father will come home again even though she cannot see him while he is at work; or that her toy doggie will still be there when Mother brings her back from shopping.

Lucy goes to her mother who is making the double bed. Lucy pulls the sheet and puts her head under it. Mother exclaims, "Oh!" and removes the sheet from Lucy's head. Lucy and Mother laugh, and Lucy covers her head again. Mother asks, "Are you helping Mommy?" and makes the bed. Lucy kneels down by the bed and pulls a corner of the bedspread and covers her head with it. Mother says, "Peek-a-boo!" They laugh and Lucy repeats the game many more times. Mother says, "Come on," and removes the bedspread from Lucy. Lucy pulls it to cover her head again. Mother puts a diaper over Lucy's head and repeats, "Peek-a-boo!" Lucy continues playing the peek-a-boo game with the diaper.

Experimentation: Christopher checks out the effect of static electricity on his hair

Reflection. Can a thing be in two places at once? This is the question posed by Brenda, as she puzzles out the concept of reflection.

Mother clips a small barrette on Brenda's hair. Mother: "You can see it in the mirror." (There is a full-length mirror on the wall a few feet away.) Brenda looks around puzzled. Mother repeats, "Look in the mirror!" Brenda moves toward the mirror, and Mother points to the barrette in her hair as Brenda looks in the mirror. Mother: "You have to get near to see it," and leads her nearer to the mirror. Mother: "See your barrette? See it?" Brenda pulls at her hair and at the clip. She still appears puzzled. It seems as if she cannot reconcile the feel of the barrette in one location (the hair that her hand is touching), and seeing it in front of her in another position. Mother fixes the barrette in her hair and says, "You are not watching. Look there!" Mother points to the reflection in the mirror, and Brenda stares, still pulling at her hair, with a mystified expression.

Light. In the next excerpt, Tommy, a sixteen-month-old boy, is puzzled by another curious phenomenon. What is sunshine? Is it a thing that creeps in through the slots of a window shade? How can it come and go so mysteriously?

Tommy sits in a chair by the window in his sister's room. He leans over and lifts up the window shade a little. He looks at the sunshine stream into the room and on to the floor. He puts the shade down and watches the stream of sunshine disappear. Tommy shakes the shade and watches intently the flashes of light on the floor caused by the motion of the shade. He shakes the shade repeatedly. His mother comes into the room, puts the shade all the way up and carries Tommy to the kitchen.

Volume.   Does a kettle hold more water than a spice bottle? Does a spice bottle hold more water than a small jar? How many jars of water does a kettle hold? Sam, like many another two-and-a-half-year-old, finds water an infinitely fascinating substance. All he needs, in addition, are three containers of different sizes, and his four-phased experiment on volume is underway.

(Phase 1)   Sam is playing "dishing" at the kitchen sink. He pours all the water from a small jar into a toy tea kettle, then pours the water back into the jar. He looks inside the kettle and finds there is more water left inside. He pours the water from jar to kettle again.

(Phase 2)   Sam fills up the jar with water from the faucet, then pours more water from the kettle into the jar but the water overflows on the sink counter.

(Phase 3)   Sam empties the water from the jar to the kettle, then empties the water from a spice bottle to the kettle. He looks inside the kettle and dumps all the water out. Sam puts some water from the faucet into the kettle, then fills up the jar with water from the faucet and pours it all into the kettle. He next empties the water from the spice bottle into the kettle. He looks inside the kettle and it is still not filled.

(Phase 4)   Sam fills up the jar with water from the kettle, then dumps it out into the sink. He repeatedly fills up the jar with water from the kettle and then dumps it out two or more times, but there is still water left in the kettle. Sam fills up both the jar and the kettle from the faucet and lines the containers side by side on the sink counter.

In the first phase of his experiment, Sam pours water in and out of the tea kettle and the small jar, and he notices that he can empty all the water from the jar to the kettle but not the reverse. In the second phase he experiments with the maximum capacity of the jar and finds out that if the jar is filled, any additional amount of water will overflow. In the third phase Sam experiments with the capacity of the kettle and sees that it can hold all the water from the jar as well as that from the spice bottle. He repeats the action to confirm his conclusion. In the fourth and final phase, Sam experiments by filling up the jar three times with water from the kettle without emptying it and verifies his discovery that the kettle can hold much more water than the jar. Sam's many-phased experimentation suggests that he is trying to understand the concept of volume. It is

not too farfetched to say that he is also struggling to grasp the funda-
mentals of addition and subtraction in as direct and concrete a fashion
as he can.

EXPERIENCING THE ENVIRONMENT THROUGH
OBSERVATION AND IMITATION

Young children spend a great deal of time watching people, events
around them, and objects that interest them. Their "watching" behavior
usually involves concentrated attention and an intense interest in minute
details. It is very difficult to know what is going on *inside* a child's
mind when he is merely observing, if there are no behavioral cues as to
what his experiences might have been. In some cases we can make a
guess, if a child *talks* or *acts* while he observes or *delays* such reactions to
the observed events until a later time.

Our first descriptive account shows a twenty-five-month-old girl
studying an ant on the playroom floor. The second tells of a boy of the
same age watching his father sprinkling seeds in the vegetable garden in
the backyard. In both cases, it is difficult to determine what the children
learn through their observation of things and people, except that they
are presumably better acquainted with what they have observed so
deliberately.

> Betty bends down to pick up a plastic block and sees an ant crawling on the
> floor. It crawls under a toy xylophone. Betty pulls the xylophone aside and
> the ant goes to a chair. Betty moves the chair and the ant crosses the floor
> again. Betty squats down and bends her head upside down to watch the ant
> crawling under her legs. She stands up and watches the ant crawling onto
> the shape-sorting box, then crawling in and out of the box. Betty runs out of
> the playroom.

> David is standing on the back porch. He looks on as Father comes out to the
> backyard with a bag in his hand. Father takes some seeds out of the bag and
> starts to sprinkle them in a small fenced-in area of the yard. Matthew goes
> down the steps, holding on to the bannister and keeping his eyes on Father.
> He is on the pavement adjacent to the dirt ground and continues watching
> Father. Then he steps into the fenced area and follows Father around as he
> sprinkles seeds.

We are in a better position to infer what the child is thinking when,
as with Tom, in the following excerpt, he deliberately copies the actions
of another. Because of his immediate imitation, we are able to tell that
Tom has observed his brother's action and also his reaction of displeasure.
In his mimicking Tom pretends to taste the berries, then putting on the

**CONCENTRATED ATTENTION
AND AN INTENSE INTEREST
IN MINUTE DETAILS**

same expression of displeasure as his brother. His vicarious experience is then confirmed, when he actually samples the berries himself and grimaces with distaste!

> Tom and his brother Dick are exploring in the bushes on the terrace in back of the house. Dick picks a white flower off a bush; Tom imitates and picks one also. Dick moves to a bush of green berries and picks a berry and puts it into his mouth. Tom watches him intently. Dick makes a disgusted sound "yech" and spits the berry out. Tom echoes "yech!" Dick picks more berries and spits them out as Tom watches. Tom starts to imitate, picking a berry and putting it into his mouth. He smiles as he tastes the sour berry, then spits it out. He looks at Dick and yells out "yech!" with a big grin on his face. Tom reaches for another berry and repeats the sequence.

Sometimes a child's imitation is not immediate but delayed to a later time. The next example shows how a twenty-six-month-old girl who, having watched her older sister practice the piano every afternoon, now undertakes to do the same in imitation.

Imitation

**MAKE-BELIEVE:
AMANDA ENJOYS
A MUD MILKSHAKE**

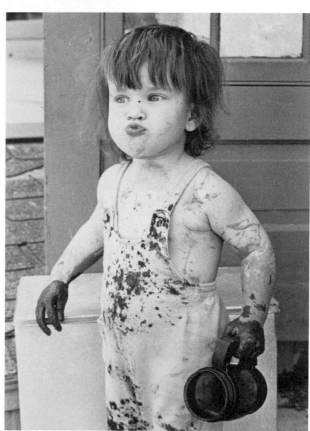

> Sally climbs onto the piano bench in the living room (where she has been observed on other occasions watching her sister practice the piano). Sally seats herself in the center of the bench and starts to "play" the piano, touching the keys at random. She turns the pages of a book of music on the piano, then "plays" the random notes again. She continues in this activity for about three minutes.

The following is an observation on Mike, a twenty-eight-month-old boy who has watched his father scolding his sister for going up the back stairs. Twenty minutes later we come upon him talking to himself and revealing the rule he has learned by observation.

> Mike walks out to the back hall slowly. He stands at the bottom of the back stairs and looks up. Then he looks to the kitchen and listens to see if Father is coming. Mike bends over, starting to go up the stairs and says: "No, no. Don't go upstairs. Get out." He then walks back to the kitchen.

We shall end this section with two excerpts illustrating make-believe play. This type of play is beloved by child-observers since it is apt to be full of weird and wonderful sayings and doings that reveal dramatically the child's illogicalities, peculiar social understandings, and emotional preoccupations. In fact, we observed only a few examples of self-maintained, *sustained* make-believe play in the very young children we observed in our research study. In most of the observations in which we suspected that make-believe was going on, the child's verbalizations were minimal and his actions so ambiguous that it was hard to know whether he was using objects realistically or truly pretending.

The following two excerpts are among the few examples of clear, self-maintained, sustained make-believe play that we came across. They lack the color and drama the reader might expect, but remember, the actors are under two years old.

> Randy (age twenty-one months) puts a long thin stick horizontally under the front of his blue overalls (between the overalls and the shirt). He starts running around in circles in the playroom and calls out loudly, "I am a bird—flying!" David holds the ends of the stick which he holds across his chest and moves the ends up and down as if flapping his wings in flight.

> Carol is playing with a basket of miniature kitchen things. She takes out a milk bottle, tries to snap the cap on, and fails. She now pretends to pour "milk" from the bottle into a tiny cup, tries to put the bottle cap on, and succeeds. Carol pretends to drink from the little cup making smacking sounds with her lips. She takes the cap off the milk bottle, takes a small plastic bowl from the basket, and pretends to pour "milk" into the bowl. She continues pouring "milk" with various containers for several minutes.

The subject of this chapter has been the child in action. We have drawn from observations of many children in our research study to illustrate the various forms of development one can see in actual behavior. We have tried to show that the child's experiences are the material from which he constructs his intelligence and personality, and that these experiences and their developmental significance can be understood and appreciated by another person through observing the child's behavior.

Careful observation and interpretation of the child's behavior in terms of some adequate framework for understanding learning processes and the course of childhood development is a necessary first step to influencing a particular child's development. Caregivers should understand, for example, that it may be the case that when a child repeatedly throws objects to the floor to watch them fall he is not being malicious but rather struggling to grasp a fundamental law of nature; when he stacks up the kitchen pots and pans he is not being bad but busy; when he imitates the actions of a grown-up he is not mocking him but learning from him; when he jabbers out an incoherent monologue in make-believe he is not acting crazy but creative.

When a mother understands that these behaviors may be mere manifestations of growing intellectual competence rather than naughtiness or stubbornness, she is more apt to accept the view that her main child-rearing objective is not simply to control the child but to encourage, extend, and stimulate his purposeful activity. She does this by recognizing, permitting, providing, and entering into learning opportunities for the child, balancing off his needs against her own and those of others in the family. How some mothers in our research study managed to do this despite striking differences in personal style, values, and life circumstances—and how others seemed to miss out—is the focus of the remainder of this book.

3

The Influence of People

People are the most important ingredient in the young child's environment. They are the most interesting things for him to watch, his most important resource for learning, the strongest influence on his behavior, the most receptive object of his love. It is true that the one- to three-year-old spends endless hours exploring his physical environment: playing with pots and pans, cars, dolls, water, dirt—any object within reach. Nevertheless, his experiences with other humans seem to have a qualitative impact well beyond their sheer quantity.

In part this is because other people can greatly influence a child's experiences without actually interacting with him. For example, the child's mother plays an important indirect role on the child's experiences merely by the way she organizes his physical environment, regulates his daily routine, arranges his access to people, places and things, and sets up rules for what he must and must not do. Similarly, she and other people in the child's world supply in themselves constant models for the child to observe and imitate. They do not need to do anything with the child, they just need to be there for him to view. In a somewhat more direct way, other people influence the child's experiences by facilitating them—suggesting things for the child to do when he's run out of steam, providing materials he needs for a project, or expressing encouragement or approval of what he is doing. Analogously, others influence his experiences by restricting them—taking away a plaything, preventing the child from doing something he wants to do, or punishing him for something he has done.

But if our research study demonstrates anything, it is that the *most important way* that other people influence a child's experiences is the obvious one—by direct involvement in the child's experiences. This stands out as the key factor significantly distinguishing the experiences of well-developing and less well-developing children.

In this chapter we shall describe many of the roles that particularly a mother plays in the experiences of her young child. We shall start with the most indirect—her role as the arranger of his environment and shaper of his routine—then move through her intermediate roles as an object of observation, as an observer, as a facilitator, and as a restrictor. Finally, we shall come to her role as an active participant in the child's activities. The focus of this section will be on the other person's behavior rather than that of the child. Our purpose is to describe—again in the concrete detail given by excerpts from our observations—the ways in which other people make a difference to what the child experiences and, therefore, to his development.

THE MOTHER AS ORGANIZER

The mother—or principal caregiver—plays an important indirect role in the child's experiences as an organizer of his daily routine, a designer of settings for his activities, and as a maker of rules governing his access to people, places, and things. This role overlaps with the mother's more direct interactive roles in the sense that we can often actually observe the mother telling the child what to do or not do ("Why not play with your cars for a while?"; "No, you may not rummage in the garbage."); where to go or not go ("Go into the yard and play"; "No, you know I don't let you play in the cellar."); when to do or not do something ("It's time for lunch now."; "No, you'll have to wait 'til after your nap to ride your trike."); who to be with and who not ("Go, see what Daddy's doing."; "Don't bother your brother, he's busy.") and so on. But unless one spends a lot of time visiting the home and focusing specifically on the mother's activities, one obviously cannot see all that the mother does in her role as organizer. For example, every mother spends a fair amount of time preparing meals for her toddler, cleaning up before and after him, picking up his toys, washing his clothes, and buying or making food, clothes, and toys for him. None of these functions necessarily involve her interacting with him, yet they have a discernible influence on how healthy, happy, alert, and curious he is. We did not study the mother's role as organizer fully in our research, but we did examine two aspects of the child's life that reflect her influence—the child's daily routine and the quality of his physical environment.

We studied both aspects by means of interviews and by asking the mother at the end of each visit to describe the child's activities of the previous twenty-four hours. We have not yet analyzed these data systematically, but several impressions already stand out. First, the typical mother cannot report her child's activities in any great detail. She can remember such unusual events as taking a trip to the zoo, or such ordinary ones as mealtimes and naptimes and father coming home from work, but usually not what goes on in between. Yet, even here there seems to be a difference between mothers of well-developing and less well-developing children in the detail that they can recall. Perhaps because the former actually spend more time observing the child and interacting with him, they are usually able to recount his activities in finer detail, often adding their own interpretation of what he was getting out of the activity. In contrast, mothers of less well-developing children describe most of the child's activities as "playing around."

Here are typical day reports of two such mothers:

Karen, age twenty-six months

When	Where	With whom	What was S doing?
Sunday, 12 noon	outside in pool	Mother, Judy (sibling), age five	water play: pouring from one container to another
12:20 p.m.	outside—Karen in a carriage	Father, Mother	walking to specialty food store
2:00 p.m.	home—own room	alone	napping
5:30 p.m.	kitchen	Mother	supper
6:15 p.m.	outside—nearby park	Mother, Father, Judy	running, learning to turn a somersault, watching Judy climb trees
8:45 p.m.	home—own room	Mother, Judy	getting ready for bed, being read a story
9:15 p.m.	home—own room	alone	asleep
Monday, 7:45 a.m.	home—own room	Judy	getting up and getting dressed, sticking gummed pictures on paper
8:30 a.m.	dining room	Mother, Father, Judy	breakfast
8:45 a.m.	stairway in kitchen	alone	playing on the stairs with a six-inch wooden cube: experimenting with the various placements of herself and the cube on stairs, e.g. sitting on the cube, then resting her feet on it, intermittently attending to adult conversation

When	Where	With whom	What was S doing?
9:00 a.m.	living room	Mother, adult visitor	playing with an old typewriter, trying to put paper in and pounding on the keys
9:45 a.m.	home—own room	Mike (visitor), age two	putting doll furniture in a doll house
11:00 a.m.	out in carriage	Mother	going along as Mother did errands including grocery shopping

Melanie, age twenty-seven months

When	Where	With whom	What was S doing?
Thursday, 2:00 p.m.	outside in wading pool	Mother, Cathy (sibling), age five	playing in water— not at all afraid
5:00 p.m.	outside	Father, Cathy, dog	running and playing
6:00 p.m.	kitchen	family	supper
7:00 p.m.	own room	alone	asleep
Friday, 8:00 a.m.	inside house	Mother	breakfast and playing
10:00 a.m.	own room	alone	nap
12 noon	inside house	Mother, David (visitor), eighteen months	playing with toys

Another way in which the typical days of the well-developing and less well-developing children seem to differ is in the types of activities that are reported. In the coding of our actual observations on these same children we have repeatedly stressed that any type of activity, however commonplace or seemingly "noneducational," may give rise to experiences that stimulate the child intellectually. A child can gain as much from playing with stones in the garden as from playing with a finely graded set of blocks. These mothers' reports therefore must be considered critically. We cannot conclude that, when Johnny's mother says he spent all morning playing with blocks, he necessarily used them very constructively or, conversely, when Mary's mother says she spent the afternoon "messing around" that was all Mary did. Although we are aware of the limitations of these reports, we feel that they must be considered nevertheless in showing certain differences in the typical experiences of well-developing and less well-developing children.

First, well-developing children are much more likely to be involved in activities of an "educational" nature—working with crayons, scissors, paper and paste; building with blocks, tinker toys and lego; fitting puzzles; modeling with playdough; looking at books; and listening to records. Similarly, they are more likely to be taken on special trips supposedly of educational benefit to children—visits to a zoo, to a farm, to a children's museum, to a library, to an airport, to a school bazaar, and for a drive in the country or a walk in the woods. These are all activities that traditionally have been thought to widen a child's intellectual horizons.

Turn now to a contrasting type of activity that is primarily adult in nature, but in which a child can share. From what we gathered in the mothers' reports, well-developing children are much more likely than their less well-developing counterparts to be allowed to "help" with household chores—cooking, making beds, dusting furniture, sorting laundry, shopping, raking leaves, planting seeds, shoveling snow, hammering nails and so on. This may be due to the fact that all the parents of the less well-developing children are of the working class and probably face more pressing domestic responsibilities. Involving their very young children in "helping" with household chores simply takes up too much valuable time and effort.

A third impression that stands out in these reports is the greater amount of time fathers seem to spend with well-developing children. The large majority of fathers of children in our research were, of course, away at work when we visited the home, so we did not often observe their on-the-spot interactions with their young children. But, from the mothers' reports it seems that fathers of well-developing children are more likely to have a close relationship with them, devoting a fair amount of time either to child's play with them or to such adult activities as work in the yard, going on errands, and sports. Often these mothers report that the child is very attached to Dad and looks forward with particular excitement to these times with him. Sometimes a note of chagrin creeps into the mother's voice, as she relates the special delight the child takes in spending an hour with his father while eight hours of her companionship are taken for granted!

We saw another aspect of the mother as organizer from our observations of the child's physical environment. Here we were specifically interested in the kinds of toys and household objects that the child had access to. As might be expected, we found that the variety, quantity, and quality of playthings vary greatly from home to home. At one end there is the case of Jennifer, the child who "has everything": a playroom with specially constructed climbing apparatus; child-sized chairs, tables, and bookshelves; a housekeeping corner with miniature stove, refrigerator, and sink; a child-sized piano, guitar, and record player with dozens of records;

books enough to stock a small library; window-boxes to see seeds grow; gerbils and fish to view animals' behavior; blocks, puzzles, crayons, paints, dress-up clothes—you name it! In poignant contrast is the case of Mike, the child who "has very little": a plastic toy radio, a couple of broken cars, a chewed-up rag doll. But most children in our research—middle class or working class—possess a fair number of toys. The major difference again seems to be in the "educational" nature of the toys and their potential for imaginative use. Well-developing children are more likely to have the kinds of toys beloved by preschools: blocks, tinkertoys, crayons, scissors and paste, puzzles, records, books; and, as we have seen, they are more apt to use them extensively. They also seem to be more frequently allowed access to household items and materials whose use traditionally is considered inconvenient, messy, or even dangerous. Playing with water at the sink, for example, cutting with knives or scissors, rummaging in the kitchen drawers, or using father's tools. But in all of this, the use of two particular objects stands out: books and television.

Take books. Although we expected a discrepancy, it was still surprising to find the very large difference between well-developing and less well-developing children in the availability and use of books. Certainly there is a large social-class difference here. In our study the typical well-developing child from the middle class has dozens of children's books at his disposal and, according to mothers' reports, is read to regularly at least fifteen minutes every day. By comparison, the well-developing child in the working class has perhaps five to ten books of his own and is read a short story or two most nights at bedtime. In striking contrast to both of these groups, the less well-developing child typically has none or at most one or two books for his use and is seldom, if ever, read to. Apparently, mothers of the latter group believe that one- to three-year-olds are not interested in books, or, if they are, they cannot be trusted not to destroy them.

Turn now to the use of television. The majority of children in our research study seem to like watching television. But what programs are they allowed to watch and what do they watch? At the one end there are some mothers who regulate television watching very strictly. The child is not allowed to turn on the TV without asking permission and only specific programs—usually *Sesame Street* and *Captain Kangaroo*—are permitted. In every case these are mothers of well-developing children. In many other cases, regulation is not an issue. The child himself is highly selective about programs he is interested in watching and there is no particular need to turn off *Batman* or *Lost in Space,* since he does not want to watch them anyway. This is true for some well-developing and some less well-developing children. But a fair number of children of both groups really like to watch TV and given half a chance would watch the

Lucy Show, the *Dating Game, What's My Line,* or whatever happens to
be on. It is here that a difference in the regulatory behaviors of mothers
of well-developing and less well-developing children becomes apparent.
According to their mothers' reports (and our own observations) well-
developed children spent much less time watching television than their
less well-developing peers and the programs they watched were much
more likely to be children's educational programs, such as *Sesame Street,*
Captain Kangaroo, and *The Electric Company* than adult-oriented programs such as the *Lucy Show,* quiz shows, and soap operas. Again we
come up against the question of quality and selectiveness.

THE MOTHER AS MODEL

The mother (or father, brother, sister, friend) can also have an indirect
influence on the child's development merely by going about her business
and letting the child observe her. Children, especially those under two,
spend a great deal of time simply watching what goes on around them.
We have no sure way of knowing what the child takes in from this
intense scrutiny, unless he imitates the observed action or tells us something about it. But we have no reason to doubt that the child does learn
from observing more mature people behave, even when he is currently
incapable of reproducing their behavior. Typical events that young children observe with avid interest are mothers and fathers performing household chores, people talking to one another, and older children playing
with toys that they themselves are yet too young to handle.
        What does the child gain from these observations? Surely, he learns
to understand that these are activities that *people* do; that they are desirable, appropriate and valuable; perhaps (and unfortunately) that certain
activities are done mostly by certain people (mothers cook and clean;
fathers roughhouse and play ball; brothers ride bikes and race cars; sisters
dress up and play house); perhaps too, he gradually learns a little about
how to do these things himself. We are very uncertain about how these
messages are actually transmitted to a child except to say that repeated
exposure (as with television commercials) seems to have profound effects
—the medium indeed may be the message.

THE MOTHER AS OBSERVER

A major theme of this book is the necessity for the mother or caregiver to
observe the child's behavior, and to interpret it developmentally. The

behavior of young children is exciting to watch and challenging to understand. Observation and interpretation are also the preconditions for effective interaction which, we believe, is the most powerful way of influencing a child's development.

Most mothers cannot afford to spend a great deal of time observing their young child's antics. They are happy when he is busily occupied on his own, so they can get on with their own chores and responsibilities. Thus, we are certainly not suggesting that a mother should take a stopwatch and note pad and spend an hour every couple of weeks, as we did, observing their child's moment-to-moment experiences. No child would let his mother do this, and the very fact that it was his *mother* observing him would distort his behavior. Something more natural, incidental, and intermittent is desirable. The trick that mothers of well-developing children seem to pull off is to be able to observe the child out of the corner of one eye, so to speak, as they go about their affairs; to observe him also while they are sharing in an activity with him in which he plays a predominant role; to listen carefully to his babbles and sayings; and further, to reflect on what they have seen. The most active and effective forms of participation in a child's activities usually do not allow time for deliberate, reflective observation; but they do presuppose a knowledge of the child's interests, abilities, and temperament gained from prior observation and experience.

THE MOTHER AS FACILITATOR

Intermediate between the mother's role as observer and her role as active participant is her role as facilitator of the child's activities. She plays this role when she suggests something for the child to do, when she provides him with materials for a project, when she permits or encourages an activity, and when she praises or approves of something the child is doing, making it more pleasurable for him, and perhaps more likely to recur in the future. This role needs no sophisticated commentary. We need only say that a young child, despite his all-consuming curiosity, often needs guidance as to what to do; otherwise his energy may be turned to badgering his mother, squabbling, or getting into danger; or it may be drained off in hanging around, whining, and flitting from place to place and thing to thing. Also, he obviously often needs help in securing materials to keep him productively occupied. Toys may be on shelves too high for him to reach, his favorite racing car may have gotten stuck under the couch and he hasn't sense or strength enough to pull it out, attractive pots and pans are hidden behind cupboard doors too hard for him to pull open. The young child also needs occasional praise and encouragement. Usually the intrinsic quality of the activity in which he is engaged is in itself enough to keep him interested, but he needs to feel that his actions are pleasing and valuable to others and not just a nuisance. This is especially important for children who have a lot of "no's" directed at them, a word that signals the mother's role as restrictor.

THE MOTHER AS RESTRICTOR

Let us begin by saying that total permissiveness was never the case in the homes that we visited in our research. All families put some limits on their children's behavior. In all homes there are objects that must not be used by small children, and there are behaviors that are not tolerated. The question is one of *degree*. Modern philosophies of child development favor greater permissiveness than traditional notions. But does degree of permissiveness actually make a difference to the child's intellectual development? We find no clearcut answer either in our own research or in that of others.

The main conclusion that our research findings suggest is that differences in the amount of restriction, the form of restriction, the object of restriction, and the justification for restriction vary primarily with social class. Middle-class mothers tend to use restriction more sparingly, are more likely to employ techniques of distraction than direct prohibition or punishment, are more likely to restrict certain behaviors such as aggressiveness and less likely to restrict others such as getting into things, and finally, are more likely to offer the child a justification for a restriction. However, within the working class there are no discernible group differences in the use of restriction by mothers of well-developing and less well-developing children. If there is a difference it is perhaps in the *consistency* with which mothers of the former group apply restrictions and their tendency to follow through to make sure that the child obeys. But even this is merely an impression gained from reading numerous observation records rather than a quantitatively documented finding. (We did not score consistency in our records.) So it is hard to come to categorical conclusions as to the mother's role as restrictor, except to say that it is clearly a question of degree, consistency, and quality and that, when restrictions are very frequent and arbitrary and punishment vehement or violent, children do suffer markedly. There were a few children in our study who encountered highly restrictive and punitive environments, and in every case their development seemed profoundly affected. One such case is the story of Vicky described in chapter 7.

THE MOTHER AS PARTICIPATOR

We now come to an area that we feel most confidence in writing about, because it is a major focus of our research whose findings are very clear. This is the mother's role as participator in the child's activities. Our research shows that the most effective way to provide intellectually valuable experiences for a young child is for the mother to participate directly in the child's activities—her key function in the child's intellectual development. In so doing she puts herself in a position to guide the child's activities in an intellectually valuable direction and to capitalize on his emotional attachment to her, in order to make the resulting experience pleasurable and more likely to be sought out by the child in the future.

To be effective the strategy of direct participation requires first that the mother *understand* what is likely to constitute an intellectually valuable experience for a child at different stages of his growth. Certainly she need not think narrowly in terms of books, blocks, puzzles, or *Sesame Street*. Rather, she should be aware that at one stage in a child's growth peek-a-boo is an intellectually challenging activity for him; at another, emptying the trash basket or sorting knives and forks is intellectually profitable; whereas, at still another stage, dressing and undressing dolls, or racing toy cars are mind-building experiences. To attain skill in understanding requires that a mother spend time watching and listening to her child in order to learn to interpret the *language of his behavior*—what it signifies for him developmentally.

The strategy also requires skill on the part of the mother when she takes part in the child's activities. Sometimes an experience is made intellectually more valuable by the mother enacting the role of teacher or helper; sometimes by her assuming the role of entertainer, playmate, or conversation partner. From our research it does not seem that any one of these approaches is superior to others in promoting the child's intellectual development. Our guess is that what they have in common is much more important than how they differ: first they put the mother in a position to influence directly experiences that may advance the child's intellectual development; and, second, they provide an intellectual rather than a social-physical context for reciprocal interaction and the growth of a positive emotional relationship. The child and mother come to *know and care* for each other in contexts that are mainly intellectually valuable rather than predominantly socially or physically valuable for him.

Participating with the child in his intellectual activities thus can have both direct and indirect effects on his intellectual development. The direct effects are those that result from the quality of specific interactions,

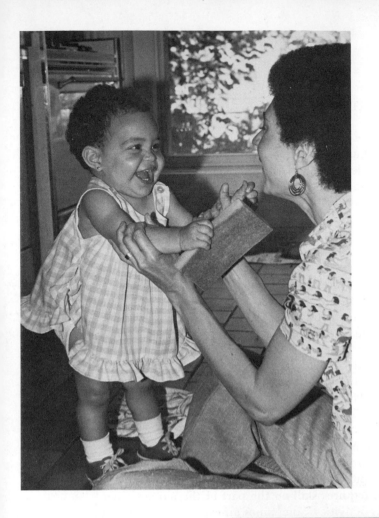

**THE MOTHER INVOLVES
THE CHILD
IN HER HOUSEHOLD CHORES**

**THE MOTHER INVOLVES
HERSELF
IN THE CHILD'S PLAY**

INTRODUCTING THE WORLD OF BOOKS

forming a pattern over time. The indirect effects include changes in the
mother's awareness of the child as an intellectual being, changes in her
understanding of how her behavior influences him, changes in her expec-
tations for what he will become, and changes in the pleasure that she
gets from relating to him. These effects are not always positive. A mother
may be so inept or insensitive an interactor that she retards the child's
development rather than forwarding it. Analogously, the indirect effects
of the mother's participation may turn out to be negative if she learns
from them that the child is irremediably "bad," "stupid," "boring," or
"difficult." It is hard to guess how many mothers may come to such a conclusion from actually participating in a child's intellectual activities, but
some presumably do. These points will become clearer in the rest of this
section as we examine the immediate impact of a mother's various participatory roles and, in the case studies, the longer term impact of these
roles traced over two years of a child's life.

THE MOTHER AS TEACHER

When a mother imparts new information to her toddler, reads to him,
shows him how to do something, corrects his mistakes, confirms that he is
right, we are inclined to say she has increased his knowledge. Similarly,
when the mother seems to help the child understand something that has
caught his interest, poses a question that seems to challenge the child, or
makes a comment that seems to add a new perspective to his thought,
the child has probably learned something that he would not otherwise
have learned—at least not at that time. These statements are made cau-
tiously because there is by no means general agreement about what consti-
tutes effective teaching, what the goals of teaching should be, or what
knowledge or learning is. In our research we use a generous and eclectic
definition of teaching. We assume that all of the above strategies may be
effective in forwarding the child's intellectual development and that they
must be taken at face value. The mother must be considered to be teaching when she does any of these things and, depending on the content of
the teaching, the child must be thought to be having an intellectually
valuable experience if he pays attention to what she does.

We shall now present several concrete examples from our observations to show the kinds of strategies included in our broad definition of
teaching. The first few accounts are in the conventional tradition of education as the transmission of information or skill by those who have it to
those who don't. The succeeding examples show a more subtle process
at work. In each of these there is a problem that seems to challenge the
child, and the adult's teaching skill consists of being able to be aware of

the child's concerns and do something that is likely to help him solve his problem actively by reorganizing his mode of thinking.

First the more conventional examples. A straightforward case occurs with Janie, age thirty-two months, as her mother tells her the names of various kinds of flowers:

> Mother is rearranging the flowers in a large vase. She is removing some and cutting the stems of others. Janie looks on. Janie picks up a glass holding one daffodil that Mother had given her. Mother picks out a carnation. Janie: "Let me take another one, Mummy." Mother replies: "Why don't you smell this?" and puts the carnation to Janie's nose. Janie sniffs, smelling the flower. Mother: "These are carnations. Not much of a smell. And those are chrysanthemums." Janie looks on, solemnly taking it all in.

Another obvious teaching situation occurs in this excerpt in which Katy and Mother are drawing.

> Katy: "Make a daddy." Mother asks, "Shall we make a body and everything?" (As opposed to only a face.) Katy: "Yeah," and grins. Mother draws. "We'll make eyes there," she says as she draws small circles. Mother asks, "Now make a nose?" Katy nods and Mother draws. Mother draws a torso on the figure. Katy calls, "Body, Daddy's body." Mother grins. "Arms?" Katy agrees and Mother draws. Mother asks, "Now a foot?" Mother draws a foot then points to the space and asks, "What about a leg?" Katy laughs. Katy asks, "Make a hand?" Mother answers, "You have to have an arm first," and demonstrates on Katy's body. "See your arm is up here and your hand is way down here." Katy looks at her hand and she smiles to Mother. Mother asks Katy, "Can you make the hand?" Katy scribbles at the end of the arm Mother has drawn. The crayon breaks. Katy says, "It's broken. Fix it." Mother: "It's all right. You can still use it." Katy begins to fill in the outline of the figure. Katy holds the crayon she is using to Mother. "Orange?" Mother: "No, it's not orange, what is it?" Katy: "Blue." Mother: "No, it's pink." Katy repeats, "Pink." Mother: "Would you like to use orange?" and offers Katy an orange crayon that Katy takes. Mother: "Would you like to make a hand with orange?" Katy draws on the figure.

Now let us turn to examples that are more in line with the progressive view of education that learning is more a question of meeting challenges and solving problems. Here is the first case:

> Father is reading to John, age thirty-three months, Ezra Keats' story "Goggles." They turn to a picture showing the dog Willy running away with the goggles through a hole in a fence. In the picture the dog's face is half hidden behind the fence. John looks and tells Father: "Doggie face broken." Father explains, "No, it's not broken. It's hiding behind the fence." John looks puzzled. He asks, "Hiding?" Father demonstrates. "See my hand. Now, see it hide when I move it behind the book?" John watches intently. Father continues, "Now, see it come out again. It's not broken. It was hiding." John

imitates Father's action several times, passing his hand behind the book and watching it reappear.

In this example the teaching strategy used by John's father is clearly more subtle and complex than those of the previous excerpts. It involves an ability to cue into the child's developmental concerns and the logic underlying his questions and to do something that helps him to grapple with a concept, if not to grasp it sooner than he otherwise would.

An observation on Ellen, age thirty-two months, illustrates the same idea, while introducing another nuance. Again, the context happens to be reading. At first Ellen seems to us to be concerned with an intellectually intriguing problem: the format of books. Why do certain illustrations appear on certain pages? What is the connection between the picture and the text? But as her sensitive Grandma quickly realizes, this is not the real point of Ellen's questions. Her concern is with death, separation, absence—interests born of a recent experience with the death of a pet cat and the current absence of her parents from home. Her questions reflect an intellectual and emotional struggle to come to grips with these ideas.

Ellen's grandmother is reading a story to her about a father, mother, and little girl. They turn to a picture showing the little girl by herself comforting a doll. Ellen asks, "Where's mother and father? Are they dead? Why aren't they in the picture, too?" Grandmother explains, "Well, this part of the story is about how the little girl found that her doll was broken. The mother and father are on the pages where the story talks about them." Grandmother shows Ellen the past pages which include illustrations of the parents. Ellen asks again, "But are her mother and father dead? Why aren't they in the picture here?" Grandmother repeats, "The mother and father aren't dead. See, they are here again on the next page. In this part of the story the girl is alone with her doll. Her mother and father will be with her later." Ellen thinks a moment and then announces, "Then we must draw the mother and father on this picture, way in the corner. Because they are thinking about the little girl." Grandmother agrees: "All right, we shall draw a tiny picture of the mother and father to show that they are somewhere else but they are thinking about the little girl. They are not dead. They are someplace else close by, just like your mother and father. Your mother and father are away, but they will be back tomorrow, and right now they are probably thinking about you."

There are two aspects to Ellen's story that are not obviously present in the previous account of John's struggle with the concept of "broken." The first is the child's clear intellectual *and* emotional conflict. (John's interest in the idea of "broken" probably also reflects similar intellectual and emotional conflicts but his actual behavior is not so clearly affective.) Progressive cognitive-developmental theory as articulated by Piaget, Dewey, Kohlberg, and Mayer points out that educative experience is experience that makes the child think—in ways that organize both cognition and emotion, cognitive and affective development being parallel aspects of structural transformations that define development.* Ellen's behavior presents a beautiful example of a parallel attempt at restructuring. Simultaneously, on cognitive and emotional fronts she is grappling with the notion that absence does not mean death and that physical absence does not mean psychological absence. (People who are away can still be thinking about you just as you are thinking about them.) Ellen's resolution of her conflicts is impressive even though it is "illogical" from an adult standpoint. The second way in which Ellen's story differs from John's, is that John's question can be answered by a teaching strategy that is entirely consistent with adult logic even though an adult is unlikely to have asked such a question. But to deal with Ellen's concern effectively the adult has to discard a more mature mode of reasoning for one that is a better match to the child's present mode of thought, allowing the child to make constructive errors. Ellen's grandmother does this by not pressing her adult viewpoint and agreeing with Ellen's "illogical" insistence that a picture must show a psychological as well as physical connection. (They must draw in the picture of the mother and father because they are thinking about the little girl.)

The need to suspend adult approaches to problem solving and to respect the child's current developmental stage is aptly illustrated in an observation of another little girl, Amy, age thirty-three months:

> Amy and her mother are putting together a puzzle. (On the cover of the box is a picture of the completed puzzle: Raggedy Ann, Teddy Bear, and Doggie having a tea party.) Amy tries to fit one of the pieces but is having no success. The piece she holds is a picture of a cookie. Mother tells her, "See, the cookie is going into Teddy's mouth, not his foot. Look at the picture. That piece doesn't go there." Mother points to the detail in the picture on the box. Amy looks briefly but immediately resumes her attempt to place the piece incorrectly. Amy announces, "It doesn't fit. It's too fat." She takes another piece and tries to place it in the puzzle without referring to the picture, apparently relying on shape correspondence and memory. Mother asks her, "You don't think the picture helps?" Amy replies, "No, it's the way it comes out **after**."

Amy is at the stage where problems of shape, size, and fit are best solved through active attempts at fitting and reliance on spatial memory. As she candidly puts it, her task is not to copy the picture by assembling

*J. Piaget, "The Right to Education in the Modern World," *UNESCO Freedom and Culture* (New York: Columbia University Press, 1951); J. Dewey, *Experience and Education* (New York: P. F. Collier, Inc., 1963); L. Kohlberg and R. Mayer, "Development as the Aim of Education," Harvard Educational Review, 42, 1972.

the puzzle pieces; it is to assemble the puzzle pieces by figuring out in spatial terms how the pieces fit. The puzzle *coincidentally* will look like the picture after she has finished it. Like Ellen's grandmother, Amy's mother begins with an explanation that is too far above the child's present mode of thought to be helpful. In the face of Amy's resistance to her suggestions her mother wisely retreats, using the occasion instead to try to understand Amy's current thought pattern by observation and probing. (Mother: "You don't think the picture helps?" Amy: "No, it's the way it comes out *after*.")

This example of Amy's mother's apparently "ineffective" teaching is deliberately selected to remind the reader of a major finding of our research: there are many other forms of positive involvement in a child's intellectual experiences besides teaching that seem to have beneficial effects on the child's intellectual development. Even apparently ineffective attempts at teaching (ineffective from an adult point of view) may help the child so long as they do not cut off the child's active problem solving. Our explanation for this is that, despite superficial dissimilarities, all forms of participation in the child's intellectual experiences share certain features: the context of the experience is *intellectual* (defined either by the child's behavior, the other person's behavior or both); the experience is *interactive*, that is mutually responsive; and the other person encourages or approves of the child's behavior. The reader should bear in mind these points when we consider the mother's other participatory roles—entertainer, playmate, and conversant.

THE MOTHER AS ENTERTAINER

For some mothers, especially those with the performer's instinct, the most pleasurable way of participating in intellectual activities with a child is to entertain him. Dramatization of stories, role playing, singing, dancing, strumming a guitar are all ways that novel material, original ideas, as well as skills involving the mastering of set sequences can be delightfully imparted. We did not often come across mother-entertainers in our research. Perhaps our presence made them feel foolish about putting on an exhibition. This is a pity, because the role of entertainer is usually received with immense pleasure by the child (and, we may add, by observers). This was obviously true for Nancy:

> Nancy calls to her mother, "Find me. I'm hiding." Mother tells her, "all right" and walks over to the closet where Nancy is standing in full view. Mother calls out in mock distress, "Oh dear I can't find my Nancy. I wonder where she's gone. Perhaps she's only gone out to buy some bread and milk, but I didn't hear the door. Oh dear, she's just disappeared." Nancy is chortling with

delight. Mother pulls back the clothing and looks in at Nancy. She shakes her head and says, "I guess she isn't here. There is a little girl here but her name is Mary. I still don't know where Nancy has gone." Nancy laughs and hides her eyes. (Presumably so her mother will not be able to see her!) Nancy continues chortling as Mother enacts variations of the theme of "Where has Nancy gone."

And equally so for Jimmy:

Mother and Jimmy, age thirty months, are sitting outside on the grass. Jimmy holds a pan and spoon that Mother has brought outside for him. He announces that he will make a cake and Mother suggests that he use some dirt from the flower bed for his cake. She watches him dig and asks what he is making. He calls, "A cake for you, Mommy." Mother answers, "Oh, yummy, chocolate?" He asks, "Do you want ice cream?" Mother replies, "What kind?" He tells her "chocolate" and brings her the pan of dirt and the spoon. Mother comments, "Chocolate cake with chocolate ice cream," and pretends to take a bite. He laughs. Mother tells him his "cake is very good" and he beams.

These two experiences are characterized by a high degree of interest and enjoyment on the part of the child and by an intellectual or creative content and a sophisticated sequencing of material. But it should be stressed that not all types of entertainment are intellectually profitable, although all are usually highly enjoyable. Tickling, bouncing, rough-housing, and playfighting are as titillating as the "where has Nancy gone" sequence of the first excerpt, but these are not the types of entertainment from which the intellectually well-developing children in our research profited. On the contrary, the group of less well-developing children more often were entertained by their parents in social-physical play of the roughhousing variety than the group of well-developing children, rein-forcing our conclusion that it is the intellectual content of the entertain-ment that is important to the child's intellectual development, rather than the mere use of an entertaining technique.

THE MOTHER AS PLAYMATE

Closely allied to the mother's role as entertainer in terms of willingness to do "childish" things is the mother's role as the child's playmate. Here, however, the mother is not so much on stage as on the floor. Her role as playmate calls for getting down to the level of her toddler and pitching into his childish but intellectually important activity. In chapter 2 we gave several examples of the reciprocal, give-and-take quality of the playmate role (remember Lucy and her mother playing peek-a-boo); but here is another excerpt that captures the child-like, reciprocal, playful character of this role performed in a way clearly of intellectual value to the child.

Mother and Jamie (thirteen months) are sitting on the floor, playing with three small plastic cups and a ping-pong ball. Mother places the ball under one of the cups in front of Jamie. She asks, "Where's the ball?" He finds it at once and laughs. Mother says, "Okay, now I'll hide it again," and places the ball under a tower of three cups. Jamie takes off the top cup and looks at Mother. Mother says in mock surprise, "What? No ball?" Jamie laughs and takes off the second cup and then the third. He laughs and Mother calls, "There it is. Hurray for Jamie!"

Jamie sees a little wooden pig lying on the floor. He picks it up and hands it to Mother calling, "Piggy, piggy." Mother asks, "Shall we hide the piggy?" Jamie smiles. Mother tells him, "I think your piggy is too big to fit under the cups. I'll get something to hide the piggy under." She shows him that the cup is too small. "See, your piggy sticks out. It can't hide under there." Mother goes to the kitchen and returns with pans for a three-tiered cake. Mother hides the pig under the largest pan and places the others on top in a tower. Jamie smiles and immediately takes down the pans one by one and uncovers the pig. He laughs and Mother claps, "Terrific." Jamie then covers the pig with the pan, but immediately uncovers it and grins. Mother: "Hey, you found the piggy. Hide him again." Jamie covers the toy pig and looks at Mother. Mother asks, "Well, where did that piggy go?" Jamie takes off the pan and giggles. Mother claps, "There he is. Hurray for Jamie. Jamie found the piggy."

THE MOTHER AS CONVERSER

The participatory role that comes most naturally and easily to mothers is that of the conversation partner. One can chat to a child while doing the ironing, or eating lunch, or walking to the bus stop. But not all forms of conversation have equal intellectual impact on a young child. The role of the conversation partner is more or less effective depending on the content and level of the language used (relative to the child's ability to grasp and be challenged by it) and on the context in which it occurs. Two main types of conversation must therefore be distinguished. First is conversation in which the content or level of the *other person's* language is such as to create an intellectually valuable experience for the child. We refer here to language used to teach (e.g., by labeling objects or events or by expanding a child's statement into a structurally more complete form); to convey novel information; to make comparisons, contrasts, and classes; to explain; to revive past experiences; to anticipate future events; or to evoke a poetic or imaginary world. Many examples of this use of language occur in our observations as in the following excerpts:

(Labeling)   Michael, age two, is watching Mother prepare cake batter. She tells him, "I'm putting in some vanilla." He repeats, "nilla." Mother corrects, emphasizing the syllables, "Yes, va-nil-la, can you say that? Vanilla."

(Expansion)

Wayne, age eighteen months, is playing with a truck on the floor near the television, tuned to a game show. A commercial for cat food comes on and Wayne looks up. He smiles and tells Mother, "Kitty." Mother asks, "Do you like that big kitty? It looks like Grandma's kitty. See, it's eating from the bowl just like Grandma's kitty." Wayne watches with full attention.

(Comparison)

Angela, thirty-one months, and her brother are about to play ping-pong. Mother brings a chair for Angela to stand on and hands her a small rubber ball. Angela announces, "Hey, this is red." Mother answers, "Yes, it's red. Your shirt's red, too. The ball and your shirt are the same color." Angela listens attentively.

(Remembering
past events)

Mother and Sonja, age two, are in the living room where Mother is about to blow up a balloon. Sonja says something to Mother about a circus. Mother tells her, "No, you didn't go to the circus—you went to the parade." Sonja repeats, "I went to the parade." Mother asks, "What did you see?" She thinks a moment and then shouts, "Big girls!" Mother smiles. "Big girls and what else?" Sonja says, "Drums!" and laughs. Mother asks, "What made all the loud noise at the end?" Sonja answers, "Trumpets." Mother tells her, "Yes, and fire engines. Do you remember the fire engines?" Sonja nods. "You hold my ears a little bit." Mother smiles. "Yes, I did, just like this," and puts her hands on Sonja's ears. Sonja laughs.

(Evoking an
imaginary world)

Sandra, age one, sits on Mother's lap. They are look-ing at a picture book. Sandra points at a picture and Mother says, "Yes, that's a dog." Sandra points to another picture and babbles. Mother tells her, "That's right. That's an egg. Would you like to eat the egg?" and holds an imaginary bite of egg up to Sandra's mouth. Sandra smiles and points to the next picture. Mother tells her, "Guitar. Can you pretend to play a guitar?" Mother strums an imaginary guitar and sings. Sandra laughs delightedly. Mother says, "Yes, marbles. Look at the colors." Mother turns the page. Sandra babbles and points at the pictures.

Sandra looks at Mother and points at a picture. Mother says, "Yes, teeth. Mama has teeth," and opens her mouth to show Sandra her teeth. Sandra says, "a-on." Mother says, "Yes, lion," and demonstrates a lion's roar. Sandra points at another picture of a mitten and babbles. Mother says, "Mitten," and shows Sandra her hand. They look at another picture and Mother asks, "Where is the owl's eyes?" Mother points at the owl's eyes, then at Sandra's eyes and labels, "Eyes." Mother points to the next picture and says, "Shoes. Shoes for your feet," and pets Sandra's feet.

The second effective form of conversation occurs when the mother makes a comment in the context of an intellectually valuable activity which the *child himself* is pursuing. The mother's comment may be fairly commonplace, but so long as it serves to convey interest in the child's activity it may be effective in keeping him engaged on the task or in imparting to him the feeling that the task is valuable. Consider the following two examples:

> Kevin has been playing with some toy cars in the living room. He lies down flat on the floor and in so doing sees another tiny car under the sofa. He takes out the new car, smiles broadly, then runs to his mother in the kitchen, holds out the car to her and chatters animatedly, as if telling her about his discovery. Mother nods and smiles. "Are you playing with your cars? Is that what you are telling me?" Kevin babbles pointing toward the living room and runs off. Mother laughs and comments to the observer. "He's always coming in to tell me something. I wish I knew what he was saying."

> Jerry is playing with some walnuts and plastic glasses. He puts a walnut into each glass then stacks the glasses into a tower of five. Mother smiles and comments, "That's getting pretty high, Jerry."

Conversation that occurs in the context of intellectual activities must be distinguished from conversation used in such other contexts as routine matters or social chit-chat. In our research, conversation used for these purposes did not correlate with intellectual development in children any more than did any entertaining style used, say, in the context of rough-housing. Here are some examples of the use of conversation for non-intellectual purposes:

> Melanie has just woken up. Mother says, "What's up Mel? Feeling good today?"

> Nathan pats a kitten. Mother, "She's a nice little kitty, isn't she?"

> Mother is cleaning house. Jody follows her around. Mother announces, "I'm going to make the bed now."

Of course, it is often a question of tone or emphasis, rather than what is literally being said, that makes a remark more or less intellectually valuable for a child who is just beginning to use language. For example, a comment as banal as "She's a nice little kitty," can be quite informative to a one-year-old if, say, the term "kitty" is made to stand out as a label, assuming the child does not already know that a baby cat is called a "kitty." Thus, in judging the intellectual value of a conversational remark, one has to be sensitive both to the child's level of understanding and to the intention of the conversation partner.

THE MOTHER BLENDS HER ROLES

We have methodically discussed the four participatory roles that mothers play in their young children's intellectual experiences; and yet we have not apparently captured the essence of the part. The fault, we think, lies in compartmentalizing the roles for analytic presentation, as if in real life they stood apart from each other. In fact, the most striking feature of the behavior of the effective participator is a remarkable blending of these roles. Read almost any of the excerpts that we have given under the four separate headings and the reader will find that many roles are combined in a single episode. The skillful participator shifts from one to another, blurring the lines of demarcation and varying his approach.

We have often used metaphors of the theater in describing the art of effective participation, and for good reason. Just as the skill of a good actor cannot be reduced to separate, quantifiable components, so too the art of stimulating and sustaining a child's intellectual interests cannot be captured by a formula. In the next chapter, as we see Matthew's mother play an imaginary badminton match with her son, she is teacher, entertainer, conversation-partner, playmate, all at the same time—although for analytic purposes we focus on only one of these techniques. Her roles are not blocked out in segments. They are combined and interwoven in a creative whole bound together by the mother's exquisite sense of her son's interests and capabilities. She challenges him to perform by performing herself; she inspires him to create wonderful images by creating them herself; she excites and pleases him by being excited and pleased herself: Like an actor at one with his audience, she closes all psychological distance between herself and Matthew. They interact.

4

Matthew and Diana:
A Difference in Skill

We have selected our first pair of case studies to show how two mothers living in quite similar circumstances and cultures and expressing superficially similar values may nevertheless create strikingly different intellectual and social environments for their young children.

Matthew's and Diana's mothers come from much the same social class and ethnic background. But they are not at all alike in their understanding of the developmental importance of certain activities for young children, in the interest they show in participating in such activities, and in their skill in promoting and sustaining them.

The intellectual and social development of their children reflect these differences rather closely. At age one Matthew and Diana seem fairly comparable on tests of development, but by two years later striking differences are apparent. Matthew at three is an outgoing, curious, intellectually well-developed little boy, whereas Diana is a shy, intellectually underdeveloped little girl. What accounts for these differences? Let us consider first the background factors that Matthew and Diana have in common.

SOCIAL CLASS AND CULTURAL BACKGROUND

Matthew's and Diana's mothers are both Irish Catholics who live within a few blocks of each other in an intensely ethnic working-class neighborhood of South Boston. The neighborhood is mostly residential except for the occasional corner store. The dwellings are typically multiple-family, cramped, and in mixed states of repair. The streets and tiny backyards are clean but dreary. There is little color about, little excitement. The impression created on an outsider is of families straining to maintain the status quo and barely succeeding. One sees few safe play areas for children, but a few blocks away is the beach, a favorite recreation site in the summer despite the heavy traffic on the highway flanking it.

Mrs. M (Matthew's mother) and Mrs. D (Diana's mother) both finished high school but their husbands did not. Both mothers are full-time homemakers while both fathers work at blue-collar jobs, Mr. M at a public utilities company and Mr. D at a trucking firm. Mr. M's income is less than $7,000 for a family of five; Mr. D's is closer to $10,000 for a family of seven. Both mothers face pressing child-care responsibilities. Mrs. M has only three children but they are closely spaced—age one, two, and three when we started our observations—while Mrs. D has five children ranging in age from one to thirteen, with two children under age three.

Given the age and number of their small children, it would probably not be feasible or economically advantageous for either mother to work outside the home on a regular basis. In any case, neither expresses any interest in doing so. They both believe that a mother's place is in the home when her children are young, and both profess contentment with the role of wife and mother as traditionally prescribed by their religion, culture, and neighborhood mores. Mrs. M and Mrs. D also have similar child-rearing values. Both believe that obedience, respect for parental authority, and getting along with others are the most important values a parent needs to teach a young child. Both feel that a parent must impart these values through vigilant discipline including, if necessary, the use of physical punishment.

MATTHEW'S AND DIANA'S INTELLECTUAL AND SOCIAL DEVELOPMENT

We started observing Matthew and Diana when they were twelve months old. Initially their performance on tests of receptive language and spatial abilities was quite similar, a similarity that continued until they were twenty-seven months old, as seen through their almost identical average-level scores on these tests repeated at roughly three-month intervals. However, on the final tests of language and spatial abilities at three years their scores were strikingly different. Although Matthew's performance was clearly that of an intellectually well-developing child, Diana's was

clearly that of a less well-developing child. Interestingly, this late bloom-
ing on Matthew's part was foreshadowed by the results of the more
general and better standardized test of mental development, the Bayley,
that both children took at twelve months. At that time Matthew's Mental
Development Index was 128, Diana's 98. At twenty-four months the
results of the same test were 114 and 102 for Matthew and Diana; and
at thirty-six months their Stanford-Binet IQ's were 110 and 83.

In general we are loath to place much confidence in tests given to
very young children before they have had ample experience with testing
procedures and the particular testers. Diana's indifferent performance on
the Bayley could have been due quite easily to her excessive shyness in
test situations that the testers repeatedly noticed up until about age two.
This shyness was quite in contrast to Matthew's eager, curious, friendly
approach, on which the testers also enthusiastically commented.

The behavior of Matthew's and Diana's mothers during the test
sessions also deserves notice. (Mothers were often used as intermediaries
in the early test sessions to make the situation less stressful for the children.) Mrs. M showed a great deal of interest in Matthew's activities
with the test materials but never tried to push him to perform. She seemed
to have a very good understanding of what could be expected of him and
accepted his success and failures with equanimity, regarding the test sessions as a learning experience both for herself and for Matthew. Mrs. D,
on the other hand, showed little interest in the tests, except to instruct
Diana to "be a good girl" and to explain to the tester that Diana might
not do well because she was tired or sleepy. Mrs. D offered this explanation almost *every time* the testers visited regardless of the time of day,
of how refreshed Diana seemed, or of the task required of the child. It
is quite possible that her remarks encouraged Diana to give up too easily;
they certainly did not help her try very hard.

INTERWEAVING THE ROLES OF HOMEMAKER AND MOTHER

We shall consider first the question of a mother's abilities to cope with
burdensome household tasks while maintaining an interest in her child's
activities. Both Mrs. M and Mrs. D kept remarkably neat households,
despite the unremittent sabotaging of their efforts by their children whose
preference seemed to be for clutter if not chaos. They took us at our word
("do what you normally do when we are not here") and spent a large part
of our visits doing household chores. But the manner in which they did
these tasks and their willingness to involve Matthew or Diana in carrying
them out were very different.

Mrs. M was typically the unflappable, well-organized housewife.

She set about her tasks at a smooth, unhurried pace, involving her boys in chores from time to time and always giving the impression that she was interested in helping or responding to them while she was doing her work. During our observations Mrs. M seldom refused a request from Matthew to play with him or help him in an activity, even though she was often busy when he made the request. This is not to say that Mrs. M usually dropped what she was doing to spend large amounts of time playing with her son. Sometimes she did this, but more often her responses were brief and calculated to set him going on his own or in concert with his brothers. She suggested new things for Matthew to do, provided necessary material or help, offered words of encouragement and interest—none of which took much time but were always supplied at opportune moments.

In contrast to Matthew's mother, Mrs. D almost always seemed harassed and overwhelmed by domestic responsibilities. No matter what time of day we visited, no matter what day of the week, we always seemed to come upon Mrs. D in the throes of doing the laundry—loading, unloading, sorting, folding, putting away mounds and mounds of clothes. Often she seemed on the point of nervous collapse staved off by a furtive break for a cigarette or a cup of coffee. Mrs. D did not welcome Diana's "helping" her with the chores; consequently she had to spend more energy preventing Diana from "messing things up." The only exception to her excluding her daughter from adult chores was an occasional request by Mrs. D for Diana to throw something in the trashcan—a request that seemed to spring more from Mrs. D's desire to distract Diana from some more exciting but inconvenient enterprise than from a recognition of this task as a significant learning opportunity. In fact, as our observation data show, Mrs. D seldom paid attention to Diana except to feed, dress, soothe, cuddle and, of course, restrict her when she got into things. The vast majority of Mrs. D's time during our observation was spent doing housework and attending to the physical needs of Diana and her preschool brother, Bobby. Despite her much longer experience as homemaker and mother, Mrs. D had not learned to interweave these two roles in an efficient, harmonious, and self-preserving manner. Seven years older than Mrs. M she looked fifteen years her senior and far less serene.

The theme discussed above is well illustrated by two excerpts from our observations that were made when Matthew and Diana were approximately thirty-two months old. First, Mrs. M and Matthew:

Matthew: Excerpt 1

Mother is doing the laundry and the dryer comes to a stop. Recognizing the signal, Matthew says, "I'll get the jammies (pajamas) out," and scrambles down from his Mother's lap. Mother: "Okay. You get the jammies out." Matthew: "Me take them out," as he opens the dryer door and starts pulling out the clothes. His brother, Ernie, runs over and they both pull the clothes out calling, "Me get them out!"

They continue pulling out the clothes. Ernie: "It's on! You better come out of there!" (The dryer has in fact stopped.) Matthew continues poking his head in the dryer searching for any clothes that might be left. Mother calls from the pantry, "Did you get it all out?" Matthew gathers up an armful of clothes and walks to the pantry. Mother: "Give them here." Matthew: "I got to throw them in here," and tries to put the clothes into the washer. Mother: "They already went in there. They're washed already." She takes the clothes from Matthew.

Now contrast this excerpt with one involving Mrs. D, Diana, and her four-year-old brother Bobby:

Diana: Excerpt 1

Mother asks Diana if she'd like an egg. Diana: "Yeah!" as she puts a toy bottle in her mouth. Diana calls, "Can we get the toaster out?" Her brother joins in: "Can we get the toaster out?" Bobby carries the toaster from the pantry to the kitchen table and hands it to Diana. Mother intercepts and takes the toaster away.

Diana: "Can we get the toast (bread) out?" She runs to the refrigerator and looks in: "Hey, Mama, where's the toast?" Mother: "I'll get it." Diana: "Where's the eggs?" Mother scolds: "Get out of there. Stay out." Diana follows her mother to the table.

Commentary.   The obvious point of contrast in these two excerpts is the fact that Mrs. M gives Matthew real responsibility in helping in an "adult" task, whereas Mrs. D restricts Diana from helping with a similar task that is well within the child's competence. This contrast is all the more remarkable, because it is our impression that mothers are more likely to involve girls in their household chores than boys; but in this case the reverse is true.

DISCIPLINE AND FREEDOM TO EXPLORE

Modern theorists of child psychology have often stressed the young child's need for freedom to explore the physical world around him, including the exciting arena of household objects. These theorists, most of whom have had little experience with running a household (especially not in a working-class context), have advocated a model of permissiveness that most working-class parents would find difficult to accept. A working-class home is often cramped for space. It cannot be child-proofed easily or redesigned to suit a toddler's needs. Working-class mothers do not ordinarily have time to supervise a child's play for very long. Thus the child must learn early not to touch things that are harmful or expensive to replace, a lesson he must learn well. The luxury of allowing an immature child to experiment with the stove, the washing machine, sharp knives, or father's tools generally cannot be afforded. But where should the line be drawn?

The difficulty is that there really is no solid research demonstrating just how much restrictiveness is harmful. In the present study we found that middle-class mothers were indeed significantly less restrictive than working-class mothers, were less likely to use physical punishment in favor of rational verbal justification for their restrictions. Among working-class families, however, mothers of intellectually well-developing children were no less restrictive than mothers of less well-developing children, no less likely to use physical punishment, and no more likely to give rational justifications for their prohibitions. If there was a difference between working-class mothers of intellectually well-developing and less well-developing children it was in the *consistency* with which the former applied restrictions and the likelihood that they would follow through to make sure that the child obeyed. These more subtle differences among working-class mothers are aptly conveyed by the behavior of Mrs. M and Mrs. D toward Matthew and Diana.

In our initial interview with Mrs. M, when Matthew was just twelve months old, she stated emphatically that she did not allow Matthew to touch the stove or open the refrigerator because they were dangerous. In our subsequent observations we found that she lived up to her word. Every time Matthew touched the stove knobs his mother restricted him, usually verbally, occasionally with a small slap on the hand. Matthew usually obeyed Mrs. M there and then, but it took several months for him to understand her prohibitions and much vigilance and effort on his mother's part. Another area in which Mrs. M was a strict disciplinarian was with respect to the squandering or destruction of material resources. Mrs. M provided her boys with food and toys in liberal quantities, but they were not to be wasted deliberately or destroyed wantonly. On this she was very firm. Consider the following excerpt taken from an observation on Matthew when he was twenty-six months old.

Matthew: Excerpt 2

The scene starts with Matthew and his mother in the kitchen. Mrs. M has given Matthew some milk to drink. Several minutes later and after several reminders to drink up, Matthew still has not drunk his milk and is mostly dabbling in it.

> Mother: "What are you going to do? Drink up your milk?" His brother, Ricky, comes in and Mother hands him the milk glass. Matthew looks on then protests as Ricky starts to take a sip. Matthew reaches over to snatch the glass but Ricky holds on tight. Mother to Matthew: "But you said you don't want

it anymore." Matthew makes complaining noises. Mother says, "You told me you didn't want it anymore." Matthew complains as Ricky drinks up the milk. Matthew takes the empty cup and looks on as Mother talks to Ricky about the big picture book he brought in.

Matthew stands on the chair and looks at the book also. Mother moves the book closer so Matthew can see. Matthew babbles something and Mother says, "What?" Matthew whines and sits on the table. Matthew babbles something about the milk in a whining tone of voice. Mother glances at Matthew, then talks to Ricky about the book. Matthew waves both hands trying to get Mother's attention and babbles something about the milk. Mother shakes her finger at Matthew and says, "No more—you said you didn't want any—you didn't learn your lesson. No more." Mother removes the empty glass.

Matthew whines for more milk. Mother: "No, you are not drinking, you just want to make a mess with it." Matthew whines, "More milk, more milk." Mother: "You won't have any more." Matthew: "I want some milk, I want some milk." Mother: "No more." Matthew whines and cries but Mother just looks on. Matthew gets down from the chair, still whining. Mother: "Go play with your brother." Matthew: "No." Mother: "Go put more people in the plane," and she goes to pick up three wooden figures and takes them to Matthew. Mother: "You want to put them in the plane?" Matthew whines, "No, no." Mother puts the wooden figures on the kitchen table. Matthew takes them and stops whining.

Commentary. To some readers Mrs. M's behavior in this excerpt may seem cold and even callous. But this was not at all the impression she made on us as observers, nor, we would guess, on her son Matthew. Her firm consistency and clear justification for the restriction seemed very likely indeed to teach Matthew the intended lesson. Mrs. M did not get angry or succumb to Matthew's tearful whining, but in her firm and gentle manner she seemed to help him save face, forget his disappointment, and move on to something more constructive.

Mrs. M's manner of restricting Matthew contrasts in subtle but important ways with that of Mrs. D. There seem to be two main points of difference. First, Diana's mother is restrictive about a larger number of objects and situations and, second, is quite inconsistent in her discipline, often not following through to make sure that Diana obeys. This failure to follow through, that characterized many of Mrs. D's interactions with Diana, is captured in the following observation made when Diana was about twenty-one months.

Diana: Excerpt 2

Diana and her three-year-old brother, Bobby, are running around the apartment. Mother has told them to quit several times already.

Diana runs to the refrigerator, then to the pantry. Mother: "Diana, stop that running! You'll fall." Diana continues running about.

Diana throws a cutting board on the floor. Bobby picks it up and throws it, nearly hitting Diana. Mother takes the board away. Diana touches a strip of linoleum on the floor and pushes Bobby off it.

Diana runs back and forth from kitchen to living room. Mother yells, "Stop that running!" Diana continues running. . . .

GETTING ALONG WITH OTHERS

Both Mrs. M and Mrs. D believed that it was very important to teach young children to get along with each other and have respect for each other's rights and property. Their success in carrying out these ideas in practice can be checked by observing Matthew's interactions with his two brothers, Ernie and Ricky, and Diana's interactions with her brother Bobby.

Actually, both Matthew and Diana seemed to get on remarkably well with their preschool brothers. We encountered very few instances of physical aggression, teasing, and squabbling over possessions. These observations were consistent with Mrs. M's reports in interviews that Matthew got along well with his brothers and her clear expectation that they would generally cooperate, share things, and have fun together despite their closeness in age and very different personalities. Our moment-to-moment observations were also consistent with the general impression of harmony, solidity, and smooth social dynamics that Mrs. M's home generally conveyed. This impression contrasted sharply with the impression of tension, friction, and unstable interpersonal relationships that Mrs. D's home often created. Reviewing our observations, it appears that these contrasting impressions had less to do with Matthew's and Diana's interactions with their siblings and more to do with their interactions with their mothers. As we have already noted, Mrs. M seemed a much more serene, firm, and consistent person than Mrs. D. She also seemed to enjoy her children more and was more skilled at handling their occasional whinings and fussings. In comparison, Mrs. D usually seemed "put upon" by her children and lacked composure and confidence in handling Diana when her daughter was out of sorts. This difference is apparent when we compare the observation on Matthew when his mother prevented him from dabbling in his milk (excerpt 2) to the following observation on Diana made when she was twenty-four months old.

Diana: Excerpt 3

Diana takes her jacket to Mother: "Mommy, go bye bye." (Meaning she wants to go out, not to take a nap.) Mother: "Uh?" Diana (yelling): "Go bye bye!"

Diana (shrieking): "Go bye bye!" Mother: "Don't scream." Diana sits on the floor and starts to whine. Diana pulls the zipper of her coat up and down, crying all the time.

Diana cries and kicks and flails about in a tantrum. Mother: "Just a minute."

Mother helps Diana up from the floor and carries her in her arms, saying, "Go bye bye later. Don't you want your nap today?" Diana, still crying: "No! No!"

Mother: "Want some cereal? Why're you cranky today? Want some cereal?" Diana: "Yes." Mother puts Diana on a chair and gets the cereal from the pantry. Diana whines, wanting to play with the box. Mother: "Want to look at it?" and pours out some cereal in Diana's bowl.

Diana whines and slides down from the chair. Mother: "Want to read this (writing on cereal box)?" Diana: "No." Mother settles Diana in the chair: "Want to see what Mommy got?" Diana cries.

Mother: "Eat your cereal like a good girl, then Mommy'll put you down for a nap." Diana wails. Diana continues crying half flinging herself over the back of the chair. Mother goes for a cigarette.

Mother: "Okay, Di, want Mommy to feed you?" Diana: "No! No!" Mother: "You'll fall off that chair." Diana climbs up the back of the chair, one leg on each side. Mother puts her legs back in the chair.

Diana continues sobbing: Mother: "Want to sit on Mommy's lap?" Diana: "No!" still crying. Diana buries her face in her hands, sobbing. Mother: "Come on, eat some cereal." (This continues for several more minutes until Diana is eventually put into her crib with a bottle.)

INTELLECTUAL STIMULATION

The most clear-cut difference between Mrs. M and Mrs. D in our observations was the part they played with respect to Matthew's and Diana's intellectual experiences. Put bluntly, we might say that Mrs. D played a very minor role in Diana's intellectual life, Mrs. M a rather considerable part in Matthew's.

Diana's Mother

As we noted earlier the demands of managing her home seemed to place great strain on Mrs. D. She seemed constantly overwhelmed with housework and paid little attention to Diana except to take care of her physical needs, occasionally to cuddle her, and often to restrict her explorations. In our visits to Diana's home there were very few occasions in which Mrs. D related in some nonrestrictive way to an activity of intellectual promise for Diana. Mrs. D's role with respect to such activities was also tightly circumscribed. She never once took the opportunity to expand what Diana might be learning by, perhaps posing an appropriate challenge, simplifying a difficult concept, or elaborating a simple situation. Furthermore, she seldom encouraged her daughter to investigate objects around her and, in fact, cut off many an exploration that might have been an intellectual springboard for Diana. Mrs. D basically seemed to show little recognition of, interest in, or appreciation of Diana's intellectual growth. In our presence she never praised any of Diana's intellectual accomplishments and, indeed, did not seem to recognize them as such. Her responses were typically lackluster and constricted. She was hardly a very stimulating playmate for her daughter.

The following three excerpts capture variations on the theme we have just developed. We start with an observation made when Diana was about nineteen months old. Mother, once again, is doing the laundry. She has taken down some bedroom curtains and the curtain rod, in preparation for washing.

Diana: Excerpt 4

Diana rubs the curtain rod on the floor and pushes it against the furniture. She chuckles to herself. Mother calls to Diana to distract her, but Diana ignores the call. She taps the rod on the door jam.

Diana scrapes the rod on the floor then carries it to the kitchen. Mother takes the curtain rod away. Diana babbles in protest. Mother: "Oh. It fell down. I'll fix it."

Diana drags one of the curtains across the floor. She holds the curtain up to the wall near the window (as if to say "this is where it goes"). Diana looks at the curtain carefully and examines a pleat, poking it with her finger.

Diana babbles to Mother excitedly, "See that!" touching the pleat. Mother does not respond but continues to fold the clothes. Diana pats the curtain and laughs. Mother: "No." Diana goes into the bedroom with the curtain. She looks up at the matching half of the curtain still hanging from its rod, and babbles to Mother as if commenting on it. Mother has followed her to the bedroom.) Mother does not respond.

Diana babbles, "Here, Ma," and hands her mother the curtain. Mother: "Put them in the pantry where Momma had them." Diana walks to the kitchen with the curtain.

Commentary. It is easy to read into an observation more than is actually there, especially when a child is unable to express precisely what he is thinking. But it seemed very clear to the observer that Diana was engaged in an important process of discovery and was struggling to share this exciting new knowledge with her mother. She seemed to be saying, "Wow! This curtain that is now on the floor used to be hanging from a window. Curtains are for hanging from windows. You use two of them and they look the same!" In a nineteen-month-old this is quite a feat of reasoning. The pity is that her mother seemed to have not the slightest notion of just how momentous a discovery this might be for Diana. She hardly seemed to observe Diana's struggle, much less to appreciate it, and she played no part in the venture except to discourage it.

Turn now to a second observation on Diana done when she was nearly twenty months old.

Diana: Excerpt 5

Mother sets Diana on the table and says, "That's a dirty sweater. I'll get you another. Stay here." Diana watches Mother go into the bedroom. Diana watches from the kitchen as Mother rummages in a chest drawer for the sweater.

Diana babbles to Mother, "Out there," repeating a phrase from Mother's previous conversation. Mother puts the sweater on Diana as she continues to babble. Diana: "Mom, that's dirty." (About the sweater her mother is putting on her.) Mother laughs, "No, that's not dirty. Your sleeve's caught up there."

Mother: "Hold up your chin." Diana lifts her head for Mother to button and straighten the sweater. Diana points to her clothes: "That's dirty." Mother: "No, that's not dirty." Four minutes later:

Diana holds up her coat to Mother, saying, "This." Mother: "After the lady has gone (I'll put it on)." Diana: "This my hat?" Mother: "Yeah." Diana picks up a scarf: "Mom, this my scarf?" Mother: "Yeah."

Diana tries to put on a mitten. She looks inside it. Diana opens up the hood of her coat that has a furry white lining and says to Mother, "This doggy?" Mother: "Is that a doggy? No."

Diana crumples up her coat on her lap. Diana: "Mom, Helen out, Helen out, Helen out, Helen out." Mother: "Yeah, Helen's going to take you out."

Commentary. In this observation Diana's mother seems to be in a more relaxed mood, smiling and responding with alacrity to Diana's babblings. But again there is the failure to elaborate, to go that little bit beyond where the child now is to enrich her experience. Diana's attempts to apply the newly acquired word "dirty" to new objects is an important learning exercise that easily could have been expanded by her mother's demonstrating which things are dirty and which are clean, how things get dirty, and so on. Merely contradicting Diana's statements by saying that what she thinks is dirty is not dirty is hardly helpful. Similarly, Mrs. D misses a marvelous opportunity later on to delve into Diana's identification of the white fur on her hood with a dog. Whether Diana meant that the white fur was like a dog's or that it was a dog we shall never know, since her mother saw only one possible meaning and did not think either to question further or elaborate her own response.

A third example of Mrs. D's failure to enrich Diana's intellectual experiences is the following, taken from an observation on Diana made about seven months later.

Diana: Excerpt 6

The scene opens with Diana and her mother in the kitchen. Mrs. D is fixing the head of Diana's doll, that has fallen off.

Mother: "Here, I fixed it," as she gives the doll to Diana. Diana tries to stand the doll on the table. Diana to Mother: "Put baby's dress on." Diana goes into the bedroom and comes back with the blanket for the doll.

Mother to Diana: "Give me that blanket." Mother folds the blanket for Diana and puts it around the doll. Diana takes the doll. Mother: "Okay, bye!" and waves at Diana. Diana walks into the living room with the doll in her arm, while sucking a popsicle.

Diana returns to the kitchen and says, "Mom, I did . . ." Mother is picking up toys from the floor. Diana says, "I'll help you." Mother to Diana: "Baby (the doll) is awake. I hear her cry." Diana goes toward the bedroom where she has left the doll . . . Diana lies in bed with the doll but hardly plays with it. Instead she eats her popsicle.

Commentary. In this observation Mrs. D does no more than she is asked to do—fixing the doll's head, folding the blanket around it—and seems intent on getting Diana to go off and play by herself. When Diana offers to help pick up the toys, Mrs. D distracts her with the fiction that the doll is awake and needs Diana's attention. In another context this might have been a very nice encouragement for Diana to engage in role play, but its real function as a distractor in this instance is, unfortunately, all too clear. Diana interprets the message as it was meant. She gets out of her mother's way but simultaneously loses interest in the doll.

We have tried to be as fair as possible to Mrs. D in selecting excerpts to compose this account. To us the conclusion seems justifiable that Diana's mother lacks real understanding of the developmental significance of many of her daughter's intellectual and imaginative activities, that she has little interest in stimulating such activities, and that she is far from skillful at doing so on the occasion when she does respond to them. This judgment is, of course, relative. It is based on a comparison of Mrs. D to mothers of intellectually well-developing children—who are exemplified in this case study by Mrs. M. It is also, incidentally, supported by a comparison of Mrs. D's relationship to her daughter and her son Bobby's relationship to his sister. Acting probably from his own need for companionship and for stimulating play, Diana's four-year-old brother occasionally engaged Diana in beautiful learning experiences that contrasted in quality with the interactions she had with her mother. We shall end our account of Diana with two examples of this play and then turn to the comparison of Mrs. D and Mrs. M.

Diana: Excerpt 7

The first observation of Diana and her brother occurred when Diana was two-and-a-half years old and her brother close to four. Diana and Bobby are playing in the kitchen.

Diana announces, "Im making supper," and puts a pot holder on a chair. Bobby joins in, "I'm making supper, too."

They stack several pot holders, one on top of the other, Diana mostly watching Bobby. Diana watches as Bobby slips a cookie under the stack of pot holders (presumably to represent the food).

Diana: "I'm making supper." Bobby: "You know what, Diana?" Diana interrupts, "You're a dummy." Diana puts the pot holders on the table. Bobby takes one. Diana: "That's mine!"

Diana: "I'm blowing my nose." She puts a pot holder to her nose and

makes a blowing sound, laughing at the substitution of a pot holder for tissue.
Bobby to Diana: "I got my teeth in." He holds a small car in his mouth
much as if it were dentures. Bobby: "Now, I put my teeth out." Diana:
"Right!" laughing.

Diana: Excerpt 8

The second observation was made when Diana was nearly thirty-three
months old. This time Diana and Bobby are in the kitchen choosing a
candy treat.

Diana: "I got black." Bobby: "Me too. Let's put them together. Let's make
a train on the couch!" Diana: "Oh?" (Puzzled.)
Bobby: "Put it together, next to mine. That's the motor in back." (He points
to the rear of the line of candies and Diana positions her candy at the end.)
Diana puts two cylindrical candies upright, like wheels, at one end of a
square arrangement, to make the train.
Diana, "Hey, you stick in—thing!" as she tries to make the candies fit
together and they fall apart. Diana: "Hey, that's a lady!" making a human-like
figure out of the candies. Bobby: "Open your mouth."
Bobby: "Put this on top of that candy." Diana does so, then sings, "On
the train!" moving two candies along the couch. Bobby: "Around the train!"
They continue this game, running around the couch and chanting, for several
minutes.

Commentary.   It is easy to see the difference between these examples and, say, the excerpt in which Mrs. D indifferently encourages
Diana to play with her doll. Bobby helps *create* for Diana imaginative
experiences, sometimes by elaborating on a theme first suggested by
Diana, sometimes by originating the theme himself, always *fully involving
himself* in the activity with her. The experiences themselves are free-
flowing, full of surprises, and intellectually exciting. Now, we are not
suggesting that a mother needs to act like a four-year-old playmate to be
successful in stimulating her young child's intellectual development. Far
from it. What Bobby's behavior has in common with that of Matthew's
mother (shortly to be described) and how it differs from that of his own
mother is, first of all, the message that it conveys to Diana that he likes
what she is doing (likes it well enough to take part in it with enthusiasm)
and, second, the intellectual leaven that it adds to Diana's own activity.
It is, of course, impossible to say whether Diana would have cooked
supper with the pot holders or made a train with the candies if Bobby
had not been there to play with her. It is also impossible to say whether
this kind of play with Bobby, unreinforced by approval or parallel experiences with her mother, made much of a difference to Diana's intellectual
development. What we can say is that our other little subject, Matthew,
who was lucky enough to enjoy such experiences both with his mother

and his brothers, seemed to progress at a more rapid pace than Diana, achieving by age three a level of intellectual, imaginative, and social skills that made him a most interesting child to observe.

Matthew's Mother

In contrast to Diana's mother, Matthew's mother seemed to be able to interweave the roles of housewife and mother with remarkable ease. She set about her many household tasks in a well-organized, efficient, and serene manner, involving her little sons in these chores from time to time, and seeming always to be interested in helping or responding to them while doing her work. In our visits to Matthew's home there were many occasions when Mrs. M interrupted her work to pay attention to Matthew's needs for guidance, stimulation, or companionship (in addition to his physical or emotional needs). Sometimes these interruptions were quite long—Mrs. M would essentially drop her work and share in Matthew's play or watch him at play. But more often these interruptions were brief: Mrs. M would suggest something for Matthew to do, provide needed materials or help, or offer words of encouragement or appreciation, none of which usually took up much time but were usually effective in engaging or reengaging Matthew in some intellectually stimulating activity.

Here are three excerpts from our observations on Matthew that illustrate his mother's ability to make herself available to him, while she carries out her household chores. These momentary interruptions from her own pursuits to show interest in Matthew's activities and to give help serve to promote and sustain Matthew's initially self-directed efforts to master intellectually challenging tasks.

Matthew: Excerpt 3

Matthew is about twenty months old at the time of this observation. He is in the playroom and has come upon a Playschool workbench.

> Matthew takes the workbench to the hall and shows it to his mother. Mother: "Right. Why don't you play with it in the kitchen." Matthew takes the toy to the kitchen.
>
> Matthew sits on the kitchen floor and tries to pull the pegs up by hand. Matthew: "There!" Mother: "What?" Matthew shakes the workbench (as if to loosen the pegs) then takes it to the hall.
>
> Matthew returns to the kitchen and shows the toy to his mother, saying, "This. . . ." Mother: "What? Where is the hammer?" Matthew: "I don't know." Mother: "Is it in the toy box?" Mother and Matthew go to the playroom. Matthew tries to lift the lid of the toy box but can't. Mother: "Want me to help you?" and helps Matthew get the hammer out.
>
> Matthew hammers the pegs with the plastic hammer. Mother moves off.

Matthew: Excerpt 4

Matthew, twenty-one months, is again in the playroom, this time playing with blocks.

> Matthew stacks five blocks into a tower. The tower falls. He places a big block on two small ones. The block falls off. Matthew lines up two small blocks then puts a big block on top of a longer one.
>
> Matthew makes a tower of five blocks, a large one at the bottom, two small ones side by side next, then two larger ones on top. The tower is solidly built and stays put. Matthew takes the two top blocks off and arranges the remaining three in a tower.
>
> He makes another tower of four blocks of different sizes. He makes still another tower of four blocks, rearranging the positions of the blocks (he seems to be trying out consciously different designs).
>
> Mother comes in: "What have you made?" Matthew looks at Mother and starts another one for her to see. Matthew: "Mommy." Mother: "What? What are you making?" Matthew builds a tower. Mother moves off.
>
> Matthew calls to his mother and goes to find her in the hall. Mother: "What is it?" and accompanies Matthew back to the playroom. Mother looks on as Matthew builds a shaky tower of six blocks, two little ones at the bottom and the larger ones on top.

Matthew: Excerpt 5

This observation was made three months later, when Matthew was two. Again we find him in the playroom.

> Matthew tries to start up a robot toy, turning the key in the wrong direction. He struggles, giving the key several turns in the wrong direction.
>
> He brings the robot to Mother in the kitchen and babbles for her help. Mother winds up the robot and they watch it "walk" across the floor. Matthew turns the key, correctly this time.
>
> Matthew continues turning the key, in the wrong direction, saying, "Robot." He looks carefully at the key, turning it in the right then the wrong direction.
>
> Matthew continues trying to turn the key, struggling with it.
>
> He twists the robot's feet and touches the key as if trying to figure out how the key controls the movement of the feet . . .

Commentary.   Mrs. M's role in Matthew's activities in these excerpts is that of a facilitator. In all three cases Matthew initiates the activity himself, wanting his mother merely to help him when he meets a difficulty and/or to validate what he has done. Mrs. M spends only a short time with Matthew on each of these occasions, but her brief help and encouragement seem to be enough to sustain his interest in the task, that he continues after she has moved away.

In addition to making herself more available to Matthew, Mrs. M's behavior contrasted with Mrs. D's on three other major points. In the first place she seemed to have a much better understanding of the intellectual value of certain types of activities. Whereas Mrs. D seemed to regard most of Diana's activities as "messing around" or "getting into things" and responded to them in much the same restrictive or constricted fashion, Mrs. M was more discriminating. She restricted firmly and consistently Matthew's investigations of household objects she considered dangerous and also his wasting of food and materials, but she encouraged his play with toys and other household objects, supplying different ones whenever he was at a loss for something to do. Second, Mrs. M seemed to us to observe Matthew's play and listen to what he had to say much more carefully than Mrs. D did with Diana. Observing Mrs. M with Matthew, one had the impression that she was thinking about what he was doing or saying and responding accordingly. In comparison Mrs. D often seemed to be excluding Diana and not really seeing what she was doing or hearing what she was saying, except as these reactions involved physical needs, whining, and getting into things. Third, and perhaps most important, Mrs. M was much more likely than Mrs. D to involve herself actively in intellectually stimulating activities with Matthew. Sometimes her role in these activities was that of a teacher, sometimes that of a playmate, sometimes that of a stimulating conversation partner, occasionally that of an entertainer. But whatever the specific variation, she played her role much more frequently and with considerably more enthusiasm and skill than did Mrs. D with Diana. The full flavor of this difference can only be conveyed through concrete example. So let us look at some excerpts illustrating Mrs. M's active involvement in Matthew's intellectual activities. First, her role as a teacher:

Matthew: Excerpt 6

This observation was made when Matthew was twenty-four months old. The scene opens with Matthew sitting on his mother's lap, drawing at the kitchen table. His four-year-old brother, Ricky, is also drawing. A T.V. soap opera is on.

> Matthew hands his pencil to Mother, gesturing for her to do something (apparently to erase part of his drawing). Mother erases the drawing. Matthew: "Circle." Mother: "No, that's a square."
>
> Matthew looks at the various drawings of circles and squares on his paper and says something to his mother (unclear). Mother draws a circle on his paper. Matthew: "Square." Mother laughs, "No, circle." Matthew (as if deliberately making a game of it) points to the circle and says, "Square!" laughing. He then points to the square and says, more seriously, "Square." Mother: "That's right."
>
> Matthew scribbles and says, "My square. See my square." Mother nods, approving. Matthew: "I'm making a square." and scrawls on the paper. Mother: "Oh, my!"

Mother makes a curved line on Matthew's paper, saying, "Draw that."
Matthew copies Mother's line more or less correctly. Mother now makes a
zig-zag line. Matthew tries to copy the zig-zag. He gets a fresh paper and
pencil. He scrawls on the paper and says: "See!" Mother nods, approving.

Matthew: Excerpt 7

A second excerpt showing the role of mother as teacher is taken from an
observation on Matthew made some six months later when he was thirty
months old. Matthew is in the playroom working on a puzzle. His brother
Ricky is doing the same and has been helping him from time to time.

Matthew takes a puzzle piece and fits it correctly. He takes out a piece he
had already put in and struggles to fit it back again, turning it about and
pushing it in. He continues but can't seem to make it fit.

He carefully turns the piece about, aligning it correctly and gets it in.
"There we go now," he says to himself. Mother comes into the room. Mat-
thew: "It's all right." Mother: "Who made it?" Matthew: "Ricky." Mother:
"How about you (i.e. didn't you do some)?"

Matthew: "There's a—right here (labeling a part of the puzzle)." Mother:
"Right." Mother reminds Matthew to tell her when he needs to go to the
bathroom. Matthew: "Yeah." Mother: "We'll go out at 11:30 when we take
Ricky to school, alright?" Matthew: "Right." Matthew turns back to his puzzle:
"That fits, right?" Mother observes.

Matthew chuckles. Mother: "What happened?" Matthew: "It breaked."
(Referring to the puzzle pieces falling apart as he tried to lift up a completed section.) Matthew tries to fit a piece in incorrectly. Mother: "No."
Matthew: "Yes. Where **does** it go?" Mother points: "This little one goes right
here and the bigger one goes here." Matthew puts in the two pieces correctly.

Matthew: "This is the one," and tries to fit another piece in, forcing it.
Matthew: "You!" (to the puzzle piece) and hits it. The piece bounces out of
the frame. Mother: "Look what happened." Matthew: "All broke, all dump
out."

Matthew fits a piece shaped like a horse. He calls out, "Me did it!" Mother:
"Good." Matthew: "Where's it go?" Mother: "Where does it go, do you
think?" Matthew: "Right here!" Mother: "Yes. Now, where does this go?"
She shows Matthew another piece. Matthew: "Right here!" and fits it in.
Mother: "Right. You did it."

Matthew: "Me did it." Mother: "Does that look right?" (Pointing to a piece
Matthew has placed incorrectly.) Matthew: "Yeah." Mother: "Sure?" Matthew
tries to fit a piece: "This one goes right here." Mother observes as he
misaligns it.

Matthew sees his mistake: "Oh no. Got to turn it around." Mother: "Yeah."
Matthew turns the piece around and fits it in correctly. Matthew tosses a
piece to one side, retrieves it and places it on the puzzle frame.

Commentary.   These two excerpts exemplify beautifully Mrs. M's
role as Matthew's teacher. Her purpose in these interactions is to help
Matthew master a skill by encouraging him to try, helping him to recog-

nize and correct his mistakes and occasionally demonstrating the correct way of doing the task in question. Mrs. M is both reactive and proactive. She responds to Matthew's initiatives and also takes the initiative herself, opening up new possibilities for him (as when she draws the curve and zig-zag for him to copy and when she points out the incorrectly fitted puzzle piece unnoticed by Matthew). Throughout Mrs. M shows a very good understanding of what Matthew is and is not able to do. She lets him struggle with a problem but not so long as for him to become discouraged. She appreciates both his off-task gaming (as when he deliberately calls a circle a square) and his on-task seriousness. She clearly enjoys both seeing him learn and helping him to learn.

A most important aspect of the contrast between Mrs. M and Mrs. D is the variety of active roles that Mrs. M plays in Matthew's intellectual activities. She is by no means always the teacher. Rather, she is flexible and versatile and moves easily from the didactic mode to others less structured, more open-ended, more imaginative. Consider the following excerpt when Mrs. M acts more like an entertainer for Matthew or a somewhat older playmate (reminding us very much of Diana's brother) than like an adult teacher.

Matthew: Excerpt 8

This observation was done when Matthew was about twenty-six months old. Matthew has wandered into the kitchen holding a child-size badminton racket. Mother gives him some milk, he drinks up, then starts to swing the racket.

> Matthew swings the racket. Mother: "Did you get it? Where did it go? Down there?" Matthew: "I got it!" and runs out of the kitchen after an imaginary shuttlecock. (Apparently, Mother and Matthew have played this game before, since her words are immediately taken as a signal to start the make-believe game.) Matthew swings the racket, hitting the imaginary shuttlecock. Mother pretends to toss the shuttlecock back to Matthew. They continue, Matthew and Mother taking turns hitting the shuttlecock.
>
> The game continues, becoming more sophisticated. Matthew seems to be timing his shots to follow Mother's and looks up at the imaginary shuttlecock each time it approaches. Matthew inadvertently drops the racket. Mother: "You lost your racket." Matthew: "Oh, I missed!" (As if dropping the racket really did cause him to miss his shot.) Matthew runs to the hallway and retrieves the shuttlecock. He pretends to serve and Mother to return the serve. Matthew retrieves the shuttelcock from the hallway. They continue. Matthew calls, "Enough, enough!"
>
> Mother: "Give it to Mommy." Matthew gives Mother the racket. Mother: "Have you got the ball?" Matthew pretends to throw the "ball" and Mother to hit it with the racket. Matthew: "No, Mommy, I'll take it." Mother gives him back the racket and Matthew swings at the "ball." Mother: "Not too close. You'll hit me with it. Stay back there." Matthew moves back. Mother

pretends to throw and Matthew to hit. Mother: "Whoopee! It's over your head." Matthew touches his head and looks up as if the ball were flying over. They start the game again. Mother: "Oh, it went over there!" Matthew runs to the hall, stoops over: "I got it!" and returns to the kitchen. Matthew: "I want a drink of water." Mother gets a glassful: "Are you thirsty?" as she holds the glass for Matthew to drink.

Commentary.   Seldom in our observations have we encountered so beautiful an interchange as the one just described between Matthew and his mother. Remember that Matthew is only twenty-six months old and has probably never seen a badminton match. Think of the imagination and skill it requires of Matthew to synchronize his movements with his mother's, to anticipate the trajectory of the imaginary shuttlecock, to retrieve it when he has miscalculated, to reason that if he dropped his racket during the approach of the shuttlecock then he has not been able to hit it. Think too of the imagination and skill it requires of Matthew's mother to inspire this performance, making their tournament evermore challenging until, at last, Matthew staggers from the court begging for a glass of water much like a tennis player after a grueling match.

The observation captures as well as any we have seen what we mean by a mother's *active involvement in her young child's intellectual experience.* Matthew's experience is profoundly developmental, his mother's behavior truly educative. She is able to help Matthew create an experience that seems to stretch his mind, his imagination, and his physical skill to their utmost. This, in essence, is what we mean by an intellectually valuable interaction.

5

Sonja and Laura: A Difference in Style

Our second pair of case studies is chosen to illustrate differences in mothers' styles of interacting with their children. We have found that, even within a particular social class, mothers of intellectually well-developing children vary greatly in their techniques of interaction. Some mothers favor a high degree of participation in the child's activities, others remain more aloof—observing the child, encouraging him, suggesting things to do, restricting him when necessary—but generally preferring to get on with their activities while the child pursues his. The stories of two little middle-class girls, Sonja and Laura, exemplify this point.

SONJA AND LAURA: INTELLECTUAL DEVELOPMENT

From age twelve months on, Sonja and Laura's test performance was equally impressive. At one year of age, Sonja's Bayley Mental Development Index was 134 and at age three her Stanford-Binet I.Q. was 142. At age one, Laura's Bayley Mental Development Index was 119, and at age three her Stanford-Binet I.Q. was 144. Their performance on our other tests of language and spatial abilities was equally precocious. On these tests Sonja ranked thirteenth and first respectively among all fifteen-month-olds in our research, and at thirty months she ranked second and third. On the same tests Laura ranked first and third respectively at fifteen months, and fifth and first at thirty months. Clearly, there was very little difference in the tested abilities of these two little girls. Yet, their human environments, specifically their mothers' styles of interacting with their daughters, differed remarkably. So we shall start at once by describing these two mothers.

SONJA'S AND LAURA'S MOTHERS

The first thing to note about Sonja's mother is that she once was a teacher, continues to think of herself as a teacher, and plans to be a teacher again. In her interactions with Sonja this sense of herself is expressed exquisitely. If the phrase "a born teacher" has an application, it is to this mother. We see here an adult who is able to communicate effortlessly with a baby of one month, a toddler of one year, or a child of four; an adult who genuinely thrills to the spectacle of a young child's development and who is thoroughly confident in her ability to shape, nurture, indeed, bring it about. Confidence, skill, delight in the performance: these are the qualities that Sonja's mother brings to the art of mothering.

Laura's mother is quite a different person. She is active in a number of political causes and civic activities, including the setting up of good child-care facilities in her neighborhood; but she does not herself enjoy all the childish games that fascinate her two daughters. Compared to Sonja's mother, her interest in her children is more intellectual, her approach more analytic. She is more impatient to pursue her professional career. Unlike Mrs. S, Laura's mother does not see her children's development as a way to express her own talents as a teacher. They must make their own music while she listens, encourages, and applauds, but composes, inwardly, a different score.

We do not wish to exaggerate the contrast between Sonja's and Laura's mothers. Actually, there are many more similarities than differences. Like Mrs. S, Laura's mother loves children and considers her presence at home absolutely necessary for their social, emotional, and intellectual development. She would be very anxious if she had to be away from them all day, and when her outside activities have seemed to interfere, she has curtailed them. She finds great pleasure in seeing Laura develop and doubts that a baby sitter would impart the values she seeks to convey—kindness, consideration for others, unselfishness, independence. Mrs. L is an extremely thoughtful woman, has read widely in the field of child psychology, and has had much experience in her volunteer work with the emotionally disturbed. She is not an armchair intellectual. She seeks to apply her knowledge to real-life problems, working hard to make a difference to other people and to her own children.

The distinction between Sonja's mother and Laura's mother is more one of means than of ends. Whereas Mrs. S really enjoys active involvement in Sonja's play, Mrs. L is more inclined to stay on the sidelines, entering in only when Laura needs her. Mrs. L participates in those of Laura's activities that she herself enjoys—for example, taking trips outdoors to look at plants and animals—but does not often share in such activities as block-building and puzzles that bore her. She is even more reluctant to involve herself in Laura's art work and creative play. One specific reason is that, as a child, she was never encouraged to paint free form but to color within the lines, and she is afraid she may dampen Laura's spontaneity. Her own mother directed and programmed her children's activities too much, in her view. Mrs. L does not want to see this pattern repeated. Interestingly, Sonja's grandmother also favored a highly programmed and directive approach. Yet, far from reacting against it, Sonja's mother seeks to reproduce it.

Although her own temperament, inclinations, and upbringing are important explanations, Laura's mother has sound didactic reasons for shying away from too much involvement in Laura's play. She feels that adult participation is valuable for the child's social development—it is one way to convey a mother's interest in the child as a person, to build his self-esteem, to get to know him, and for the child to get to know his mother. But, generally speaking, the child is the best judge of the design of his own activity. There is usually a good reason for his wanting to do a certain activity in a certain way. The child is intrinsically motivated to play in a way that furthers his own development (assuming an interesting and reasonably unrestrictive environment) and will match his play to his developmental needs.

How thoroughgoing is Mrs. L's noninterventionist philosophy? Again, we must be careful not to exaggerate. Laura's mother makes a critical distinction between verbal interactions and other activities. She considers it very important that a mother talk with and read a great deal to a child (she spends over one hour every day reading to Laura) and does not think that television is an effective substitute. Significantly, she feels confident that her contribution in verbal interchange makes a difference to Laura's language development (she is highly educated and now talks to Laura, age three, as if talking to an adult) but is much less sure of what she has to offer in spatial and artistic activities. Not knowing how she can make a difference to the intellectual value of these activities for Laura, she applies a hands-off approach as the lesser of two evils. She concedes that enlightened participation in all types of child's play might be beneficial to the child but she fears to get out of her element.

A major difference then between Laura's mother and Sonja's mother is one of confidence in their roles as teachers. Sonja's mother knows she is an excellent teacher. She has run a playgroup for young children at her home for several summers with great success. Her house is a mecca for children of many ages who come to talk and play with *her,* not just her own children. She is sure that her methods are successful (not with all children, but with many), and she has arrived at them, not intellectually, but intuitively and through experience. She goes out of her way to create a child-oriented, interesting, active, responsive environment. Her children have many options and a variety of models to imitate. They don't hang around waiting for things to happen, nor are they forced into participation. But with such activities as painting, drawing, dancing, and singing almost constantly going on, the child naturally joins in or starts one of his own.

Adult participation can expand the content of a child's activity, enrich it, make it more enjoyable, but Sonja's mother does not believe that Sonja gets more out of interacting with her than from pursuing a similar activity on her own. She is, in fact, most pleased when Sonja chooses and sustains her own play. On the other hand, she does not see her enlightened brand of participation as intrusive or unnecessary. She feels that by interacting enthusiastically with evident enjoyment, a mother directly shows the child that the activity is worthwhile and interesting and motivates her child to pursue it for its own sake. This personal conclusion on Mrs. S's part is strongly supported by the results of our research and her methods clearly seem to work in Sonja's case. Our observations on Sonja are saturated with intellectual activities pursued both with her mother and on her own, and there is every evidence that her mother's high degree of participation whets the interest of this little girl in intellectual pursuits.

SOCIAL CLASS AND CULTURAL BACKGROUND

Sonja

When we first started observing Sonja, the family lived in a nine-room house in a residential section of a town near Boston. The immediate neighborhood was entirely residential, consisting of older but well-kept, well-spaced, single-family houses. A few blocks away was a main street with stores and easily accessible transportation. We visited Sonja in this home for several months. The family then moved, but this makes little difference to our story, because the move was to a similar house in a similar neighborhood.

The impression created by both of Sonja's homes is of a messy but exciting nursery school. Central to both is a large playroom filled with masses of books, toys, musical instruments, children's equipment, and pets, plus generous amounts of household clutter. For example, in the first house, the playroom is the first room the observer sees as she enters. Hanging from the ceiling is a rubber tire for swinging; in the middle is a huge, homemade playhouse, and just outside the window a swing and jungle gym set. The second house even improves on the first by having outside a marvelous twenty-foot slide built by Sonja's father, and an intricate "catwalk," in addition to run-of-the-mill swings and monkey bars.

Both houses express a major interest of Sonja's parents, namely, children. Her mother, as we know, is a teacher, her father, an architect. Both parents have graduate college degrees, her mother an M.A., her father a Ph.D. It is this high level of educational attainment rather than residence or income that classifies the family as middle class, as in fact, the total family income is under $7,000 and varies with the ups and downs of Mr. S's free-lance work. Even so, the house is marvelously well designed to stimulate a child's curiosity, and what cannot be bought is borrowed from the library or homemade (a task for which both parents' training and interests are excellently suited).

The person with whom Sonja spends most time is her mother, but her father is home more often than is typical for fathers in our study, and we have observed her several times in his charge. Sonja also spends a lot of time with her sister and brother, who are two and three years older than she. There are constant visitors to the home and, because Sonja is also often taken outside and into the neighborhood, she has an active and varied social life. Her mother's religious and ethnic background is Jewish; her father is a Northern European of Protestant background who first came to the United States to do his graduate work at a major university.

Laura

Laura lives in an apartment in a three-family house in an "academic" neighborhood. The neighborhood is entirely residential and is not far from a playground and the banks of a river. The apartment is on the third floor and has five rooms, including a bedroom that Laura shares with her sister, Jennifer. It is furnished quietly and tastefully and kept neatly, despite the inevitable disorder caused by two lively girls. The girls' room serves as both bedroom and playroom and is furnished with shelves and baskets stocked with toys, but there is not quite the abundance of playthings and equipment that overflow Sonja's house. An observer gets the impression that a clear balance between the needs of adults and children has been struck and that time and effort are spent to keep it so.

Both of Laura's parents are college educated. Her mother attended a well-known Eastern women's college as an undergraduate and her father has a Ph.D. in physics and teaches at a local university. Her mother is of Catholic, Italian background and her father of British, Protestant origin.

The person with whom Laura spends most time is her mother; in fact, we never saw Mr. L during our visits, which is not surprising because he normally only sees the children before 9:00 a.m. and in the late evening daily, and on weekends. Apart from this difference in amount of time spent with their fathers, Laura and Sonja have similarly active and varied social lives. Laura spends much of her time with her sister, Jennifer, and regularly plays with her cousins, one of whom is the same age. Her mother and aunt frequently baby-sit for each other's children.

Laura's mother is active in a number of political causes, including voter registration and political canvassing. In addition, she does regular volunteer work in the field she means to make her career, psychiatric social work, and has taken evening courses for credit at a local university.

OBSERVATIONS ON SONJA AND LAURA

We shall start with excerpts from our first observations on Sonja and Laura, made when they were both about thirteen months old.

Sonja: Excerpt 1

The scene opens with Sonja, age thirteen months, Mother, and Father in the kitchen. Sonja is having lunch.

> Sonja drinks some milk from a cup that Mother holds for her. Sonja: "Ca."
> Mother: "Cup." Sonja: "Cup." Mother: "Drink your milk, Sonja."
>   Mother: "Is it good?" Sonja smiles. Mother holds the cup to Sonja's mouth.
> Sonja babbles, "Cup." Mother: "Cup." Mother puts the cup on the counter.
> Sonja: "Da. Da." (Pointing to a doll.) Mother: "Give the dolly a big hug."
> Sonja smiles. Mother: "Doll." Sonja: "Doll." Mother: "Love your egg? It's a
> good egg." Sonja: "Doll," and picks up the doll, then puts it on her head.
>   Sonja: "Doll." Father shows Sonja both the front and the back of the doll
> and Sonja laughs, saying, "Doll, doll, doll." Mother: "No more egg?" Sonja
> shakes her head, "no." Sonja fondles the doll, then listens to her father crack
> an egg at the counter. Sonja says "Oooh," excitedly, and reaches for the
> eggshell. Sonja touches the doll. Father gets up and leaves the room. Mother
> holds the cup for Sonja to drink more of the milk.
>   Mother: "Okay, Sonja, that's it for you." Mother brings over a towel, saying,
> "You can come out (of the highchair) now." Mother wipes Sonja's face and
> mouth. Sonja laughs. Mother: "Wash your tongue, wash your nose, wash
> your neck, wash your hands, wash your fingers, dry your fingers," as she does
> each of these actions in turn. Mother hands Sonja the doll, saying, "Dolly's
> getting dirty from the milk."
>   Mother: "Let's go. Up." She picks up Sonja and carries her into the living
> room and then into the backyard. Mother sets Sonja down on the ground and
> immediately says, "See the flowers," pointing to some roses in the garden.

Laura: Excerpt 1

Mother is reading the newspaper in the kitchen. Laura goes to her and Mother glances at Laura. Laura pushes a chair to the sink counter and climbs on it. She kneels on the chair. Mother says, "Laura, no! I thought we made a rule about those chairs." Mother goes to put her down and moves the chair back to the table. Laura looks at the open drawer of the sink cabinet. Mother says: "You can play with things in there."

Laura goes and pulls out a bib, then a pot lid. Mother looks on. Laura looks at the reflection of herself in the lid, puts her face against it, gently rubs her face on it, then mouths the handle of the lid. Mother glances at Laura, then turns her attention back to her paper. Laura puts the lid down, holds it again in one hand, and pulls out a pie pan from the drawer with her other hand. Laura babbles "eh eh," as she notices an apron string tangled with the pie pan. She stands, lifts the pie pan up, shakes it, disentangling the string, then puts it back on the floor. She sits down again, picks up the lid, and mouths the handle again. She puts the lid down and picks up the pie pan, but the bottom falls out leaving only the ring.

Laura puts the ring over her head and tries to pick up the bottom part with one hand—without success. She tries again. She now uses both hands and picks up the bottom of the pie pan. She tries to fit it back into the ring, but drops it. She pulls herhelf up holding the drawer, but slides down again. Now she is in a kneeling position. She gets up and pulls out an apron from the drawer. She drops it on the floor and picks out a can of playdough. She looks at the can, turning it around in her hands to look at the bottom. She turns it around again.

Mother is making coffee at the stove and glances at Laura. Laura puts the playdough down and pulls out another pot lid and drops it on the floor. Mother goes to make a phone call and glances at Laura. Laura drops the pot lid and watches it bouncing and flipping over. She repeats this action. Mother looks on as she waits at the phone. Laura bounces the pot lid and makes loud noises again. She babbles and bangs the lid on the floor. She makes an "oh" sound and picks up the playdough to show Mother. Mother doesn't see—her back is to Laura. Now Laura tries to open the playdough can.

Laura laughs. She picks up the pot lid and drops it repeatedly. Mother glances at Laura from time to time, as she waits on the phone. Laura bounces the lid and makes it flip over again and again. Mother looks on. Laura gets up to pick up the other lid and bounces it too. Laura picks up the playdough can and turns to Mother calling, "Mama." Mother answers, "What Laura?" as she hangs up the phone and sits down at the kitchen table. Laura goes to Mother with the playdough.

Commentary. One should not make too much of an initial observation, since the situation is unfamiliar to both mother and child and their behavior may not be truly characteristic. However, the obvious contrast in Mrs. S's and Mrs. L's styles of interacting and the difference in sheer amount of verbal stimulation in these two excerpts are, by no means, unique to this pair of observations.

Sonja's mother spends almost all the time conversing with Sonja, labeling things for her in a redundant fashion appropriate to a thirteen-month-old little girl. Sonja learns each new word and practices it eagerly. (Sonja: Ca. Mother: Cup. Sonja: Cup. Sonja: Da. Mother: Doll. Sonja: Doll.) Sonja's mother also challenges her ability with words she can't yet distinguish (Mother: Wash your *tongue,* wash your *nose,* wash your *neck* . . .). Sonja is bathed in words, words are given precise and concrete meanings, and each attempt at verbal mastery is immediately reinforced.

Laura's experience is quite different. Almost all of her activity is self-initiated and self-sustained and her mother interacts only to restrict her from climbing up on the chair, to distract her to play with the pots and pans, and then to observe her antics with the pot lid. This relative lack of adult participation does not prevent much of Laura's activity from being purposeful, systematic, and inventive. This child seems quite capable of developing fine motor and spatial skills and constructing her own rudimentary concepts about the physical world without specific guidance from her mother. The next sets of excerpts, three on Sonja followed by three on Laura, further illustrate this point.

Sonja: Excerpt 2

The observations begin with Sonja, her mother, her mother's friend, and their dog strolling about in the sunshine in the park opposite their home. Sonja is eighteen months old.

Sonja walks over toward her mother and looks around. Mother hands Sonja a Snoopy-dog pull-toy. "You want to walk your little dog?" Sonja reaches, Mother takes it back and disentangles a set of colored plastic keys from the dog. Sonja calls, "Keys," and Mother hands them to her. Sonja holds out a piece of apple she's carrying, and says, "Apple." Mother repeats, "Apple." Sonja puts it in Mother's hand. Mother holds the apple to Sonja's mouth, but Sonja turns away. Sonja falls and looks up at the observer. Mother leans over and kisses Sonja. Mother: "You want to get up?" and helps her up.

Mother pats Sonja on the head. Sonja says, "Keys," and holds them up. Mother repeats, "Yes, keys." Sonja points to her Snoopy-toy and says, "Dog." Mother repeats, "Dog." Sonja follows close behind Mother and watches as Mother throws a stick to their pet dog. Sonja stands, watching Mother playing fetch with their dog, Blackie. Mother: "Shall we see if she (the dog) can do it (fetch)? See," and throws the stick. Sonja laughs, watching the dog retrieve the stick. Mother: "Here comes another dog." Sonja moves a few steps closer.

Sonja watches. Mother: "See Blackie catch?" Sonja watches, calls out "dog" and Mother repeats "dog." Mother is watching the dog scampering about. Sonja holds up the keys and calls "keys." Sonja falls down, calls "red." Mother looks. "Yeah, red keys. Right." Sonja goes over to Mother and says, "White." Mother repeats, "Yes, white," and smiles. Sonja labels "white" and Mother repeats "white." Sonja fingers the piece of string. Mother comments, "That's string." Sonja: "Red."

Sonja repeats "red" and Mother repeats "red." Sonja fingers a white key saying "white" and Mother repeats "white." Sonja holds up a key, looking at it and says, correctly, "green." Sonja repeats, "Green." Mother is talking with a friend and looking at the dogs and apparently doesn't hear. Sonja says "red." Mother looks down, saying: "Red, I see it, Sonja." Sonja starts out running across the grass. She looks back over her shoulder and calls out "dog." Mother is talking to her friend and doesn't hear.

Sonja calls out "key," then "dog" (trying to get Mother's attention). Mother says, "Dog, yes." Sonja looks at the observer. Sonja looks at the dog and says, "Dog." Mother: "Yes, I see the dog." Sonja. "Dog." Mother: "Yes." Sonja stands, holding the keys, looking around, saying "dog," then "boy." Mother: "Yes, the boys are playing. (A group of children are playing in an adjacent playground.) Yes, many children are playing." Sonja looks on, holding the keys. She says "red" and walks toward Mother, then says "play." Mother: "Yes, they're playing." Sonja says something. Mother: "What? Oh, what happened? The stick broke, is that it?"

Mother: "That's okay; shall we find another stick? Come on, let's see if we can find another." Sonja follows Mother. (Mother's attention is interrupted by kids throwing rocks.) Mother picks up a stick: "Here's one. Want this big one?" Sonja takes it and smiles. Mother: "Throw it," Sonja throws it down on the grass. Mother says, "Oh, it's too big. Let's break it and make it **little.**" Mother throws the stick for the dog and Sonja watches. Sonja repeats after Mother, "Blackie." (The dog's name.) Sonja picks up a small piece of stick and one of the dogs comes running out and grabs for it. Mother: "He won't hurt you. Don't worry. You'll just have to try it. Here, you throw it."

Sonja throws the stick down, then picks it up and throws it again. Mother retrieves the stick, saying, "Get it, Blackie!" Sonja watches, delighted as the dog jerks the stick. Mother: "Try it again, Sonja." Sonja picks up the stick and throws it. Mother: "Get it, Blackie!" Sonja: "Black, black." Sonja watches as the dog gets the stick. Sonja looks at the keys again and says "keys." Mother: "I see your keys." Sonja says "white." Mother: "mmmm." Sonja: "ing." Mother: "Yes, that's a string." Sonja runs toward Mother saying, "Run." Mother replies, "Yes, you're running," as Sonja starts off down a little hill. Then Mother calls, "Come, run this way, Sonja, there's (broken) glass there."

Sonja: Excerpt 3

We come upon Sonja standing in the hallway, watching her brother and his friend going outside to play. Sonja is now twenty-four months old.

Sonja watches the boys go out. Sonja says, "I want to go outside," and whines. Mother doesn't respond. Sonja cries wanting to go out, too. Mother: "Michael is going out but I'm going to put on a record for you. You know why? You see, your nose is dripping and you have a little cold, so you'll be staying in." Mother picks up a balloon from the floor: "Do you want me to blow up your balloon for you?" Mother gives Sonja a large balloon. Mother, looking out, says, "They got across the street." Sonja: "Where's the stick (for the balloon)?" Mother: "Hmm, I don't know."

Sonja watches Mother look for the stick. Mother: "I'll blow it up first and then we'll find the stick." She takes the balloon and walks into the study and sits down. Sonja follows. Sonja says something about a circus. Mother: "No, you didn't go to the circus—you went to the parade." Sonja: "I went to the parade." Mother: "What did you see?" Sonja: "I saw ——." Mother: "What?" Sonja: "Big girls." Mother smiles. "Big girls and what else?" Sonja: "Drums!" Mother chuckles. Sonja laughs, as if remembering the parade. Mother blows up the balloon. Mother: "What made all the loud noise at the end?" Sonja: "Trumpets!" Mother: "Yes, and fire engines. Do you remember the fire engines?"

Sonja: "You hold my ears a little bit." Mother: "Yes, I did, just like this," and demonstrates, holding Sonja's ears. Sonja says something. Mother: "What were you eating?" Sonja: "Popcorn!" Mother chuckles. Mother blows up the balloon. Mother: "Yes, you were sharing it with Nina and Michael." Sonja sits on the floor and kicks her feet. Sonja picks up a book. "What is this?" Mother: "It's called **Dial an Alphabet.**" Sonja repeats. Sonja turns a dial in the book. (The dial turns to different letters with appropriate pictures of an apple, boy, cat, etc. corresponding to the letters A, B, C. . .)

Mother: "There's a four—1, 2, 3, 4," pointing to a cluster of four objects and the number '4' on another page of the book. Sonja looks at the book and turns the dial. Sonja: "What's this?" (Pointing to the part where the arms of the dial meet.) Mother: "That's a part of the dial, so you can turn it." Sonja turns the dial and asks, "What's this?" Mother doesn't answer as she is blowing up the balloon. Sonja repeats, "What's this?" Mother: "Another one." Sonja: "Oh, balloon." Mother: "This isn't easy, you known." Sonja watches and pats the red and white polka-dotted balloon as Mother continues to blow it up.

Sonja. "Spots." Mother: "Yes, white spots." Sonja: "Big." Mother: "Yes, it's very big." Sonja: "Are you blowing up my balloon? Are your blowing up my drum?" Mother: "Your drum?" Sonja: "No, my balloon." Mother: "Your balloon—yes I am." Sonja sneezes. Sonja picks up a book while Mother blows up the balloon. Sonja: "I'm going to read this. What's this book?" Mother: "It's about jet planes. Jets and rockets." Sonja repeats. Sonja talks to herself as she looks at the book. Mother looks on.

Sonja babbles about the book and Mother watches her. Sonja picks up another book. "What's this one?" Mother: "A book of fairy tales." Mother suggests, "You tell me a story." Sonja opens the book, looks at it, and sings. Sonja points to a picture: "Queen." Mother: "Yes, that's a queen and that's a king." Sonja: "What's this?" Mother: "It's a king looking at himself in a mirror." Sonja: "What is it?" Mother: "A man." Sonja: "A man and a man." (Pointing at the king and his reflection.) Mother watches Sonja, chuckling.

Sonja babbles about the book. Sonja talks about the book, announcing, "I'm going to read it." Sonja points to pictures of coins in the book. "That's money." Mother: "You're right." Mother ties the balloon. Sonja points to a picture: "What is it?" Mother: "That's a loom, they're weaving some material, some cloth on the loom." Sonja looks at another picture. "I don't want to read this story." Mother: "Okay." Mother bats the balloon in the air. Sonja: "Oh, it's so big."

Sonja: "Where's the stick?" Mother: "I don't know where it is. I'll try to find it and you can play with the balloon while you're waiting." Mother bats the balloon to the other side of the room. Sonja crawls after it. Sonja calls "balloon" and says, "I went to the circus." Mother: "Not the circus—now where did you go?" Sonja looks at Mother in the hallway: "I go ——." Mother: "To the parade." Sonja: "Parade! I ate popcorn." Mother: "It was like a circus, it was so much fun and there were animals there, too, remember?" Sonja: "Yeah," smiling.

Sonja: Excerpt 4

Sonja, here, is thirty months old. She is engrossed in one of her favorite activities—block building. Her blocks are red, white, and blue and have little knobs enabling them to lock together. Sonja has made a tower of red blocks and a tower of white blocks, side by side, each about twenty-four inches tall, and now she starts a blue one. Mother is in and out of the room, cleaning up.

Sonja puts three blocks, one on top of the other, to start the tower. She takes apart an already assembled set of three blue blocks, then adds each separately to the tower. Sonja to Mother: "Here are the blues. Here." (Pointing to her tower.) Mother observes. Sonja takes apart another group of three blocks and adds each to the tower. Sonja says something to Mother about the tower. Mother smiles and leaves the room. Sonja continues building, talking aloud to herself, too softly for the observer to understand.

Suddenly, she calls out, "Take a blue! Now, take a red! Now, take a white!" As she does this, she alternates the red, white, and blue blocks, dismantling the red and white towers as she uses up the blocks on the new three-color tower. Mother has reentered the room and looks on attentively. Mother praises, "Wonderful!" Sonja continues building and singing out happily each step she plans to take. "Now take all the blues . . . now take a red. . ." Sonja to Mother: "They (the other towers) are getting smaller." Mother: "Yes, they are getting smaller as you take them all away." Sonja continues to sing out, melodiously, "Take a blue! Take a white! Take a red!" (Placing the blocks in a perfect, alternating pattern.)

Sonja continues buliding and singing. Mother: "You're singing!" Sonja smiles and continues, "red, blue, white," as she alternates the blocks. Mother observes her throughout, very amused. Mother leaves. Sonja continues alternating the blocks and singing out the colors as she places them. Sonja continues with this activity while Mother comes in and out of the room busy with her chores.

Sonja continues chanting and building, absorbed in the task.

Sonja's tower is now at about her eye level and the red, white, and blue blocks are no longer perfectly alternated, but the idea is still there. Now she calls out, "Red, red. Red-red-red-red-red! Blue. Blue. Blue-blue-blue-blue-blue! White. White. White-white-white-white-white!" chanting and beaming at the observer. Sonja says to Mother who is now in the room, "See me!" Mother pretends great surprise (by way of praise) at the height of the tower. Sonja: "Don't lift it up." Mother: "Why not?" Sonja: "It's going to fall."

Mother: "I think it's taller than you are. No You are taller." Mother moves Sonja over close to the tower, measuring its height against her. Mother: "You are this much taller than it (demonstrating a length of about three inches with her hands). It comes up to here. To your eyes." Mother demonstrates by moving her hand horizontally from the top of the tower to Sonja's eyes.

Commentary.   In these excerpts Sonja's mother is very much the teacher. She loses no opportunity to reinforce words that Sonja has already acquired but is still practicing (excerpt 2, Sonja: Keys. Mother: Keys. Sonja points to Snoopy toy dog: Dog. Mother: Dog.), and to introduce new ones (excerpt 3, Sonja points to picture: Queen. Mother: Yes, that's a queen and that's a king.), even some that are clearly beyond the child's comprehensions (excerpt 3, Mother: There's a loom. They're weaving some material, some cloth on the loom.). She is constantly expanding Sonja's concepts. (Recall excerpt 4 when Mother demonstrates what "taller than" means in relation to the tower that Sonja has just proudly built.) She encourages Sonja to remember and relate events (excerpt 3, Sonja: I went to the parade. Mother: What did you see? Sonja: I saw drums. Mother: "What else? Sonja: Big girls. Mother smiles: Big girls, and what else? Sonja: Drums. Mother chuckles, Sonja laughs as if remembering the parade. Mother blows up a balloon. Mother: What made all the loud noise at the end? Sonja: Trumpets. Mother: Yes and fire engines. . .). She helps Sonja to interpret the events taking place around her (excerpt 2, Sonja: Boy. Mother: Yes, the boys are playing. Many children are playing.) and to understand the pictures in her story books (excerpt 3, Sonja: What's this? Mother: It's the king looking at himself in the mirror. Sonja: What it it? Mother: A man. Sonja: A man and a man, pointing to the king and his reflection in the mirror.). Sonja's mother provides numerous settings for Sonja to generate her own wonderful ideas and expresses open, unabashed delight when these occur (as in her response to Sonja's marvelous tri-color tower). Above all, she listens to Sonja, notices her, praises her, laughs with her, and delights in her. Sonja's mother behaves like a sister, close enough in age to Sonja to genuinely enjoy her childish activities, and, at the same time, like a teacher, whose forethought and flair constantly cause exciting things to happen "spontaneously." Like Matthew's mother of the previous case study, Mrs. S is an expert at blending her roles.

To do all these things takes time. So it is hardly surprising to find that Sonja's mother devotes many of her waking hours to activities with Sonja and her brother and sister. In each of the excerpts we have selected she spends over half the time directly involved in some activity with Sonja, whether this takes the form of teaching her the concept of "taller than," or sharing a game of "throw and fetch," or conversing with her about the excitement of the parade. Mrs. S is also a very permissive mother. This is not to say that she gives in to Sonja's demands. Rather, conflicts between her and Sonja seldom seem to arise, possibly because so few things are prohibited. In our observations we came across no more than two or three instances in which Mrs. S restricted Sonja, and no instance in which she was scolded or punished—a remarkable achievement in a relationship with an active and determined toddler!

In comparison with Sonja's mother, Laura's mother is much less of a talker, much less of a teacher, much less of a participant in child's play. This difference in style emerges inescapably as we compare our observations on Sonja to some on Laura, made when both children were approximately the same age.

Laura: Excerpt 2

Laura is nineteen months old in this observation—and intrigued by shoes.

> Laura babbles, "Shoes." Mother: "We're not going to go out right now, Laura. Put your shoes on." Laura goes to the closet in her bedroom. Laura: "Shoes." Laura takes out a pair of her sister's shoes and carries them to the kitchen.
> Laura puts the shoes on a stool, climbs up and sits beside them. Laura's sister, Jennifer says, "Don't put on my shoes." Laura: "My shoes." Mother (laughing): "They're not your shoes." Laura: "Ca ca's shoes." Jennifer: "Those are Ca ca's shoes." Laura: "My shoes." Laura puts a shoe on her foot. Jennifer: "You look funny." Laura puts the shoe on and walks around.
> Jennifer: "Laura, it's on the wrong foot." Mother: "You look funny, Laura." Laura walks to the dining room, wearing the shoe. Laura walks to the kitchen with the shoe. Jennifer: "You're doing that so you'll be recorded with that shoe." (Jennifer looks meaningfully at the observer.) Laura climbs on a stool, holding the other shoe and saying, "Mine, mine." Laura plays with the shoe, turning it around.

Laura: Excerpt 3

The scene opens with Laura's mother taking her mid-morning coffee and cigarette break. Laura is twenty-four months old and fascinated by handbags.

> Laura opens Mother's bag and looks inside. She takes out pencils, pen, notebook. She asks, "What's in there?" as she rummages through the bag.
> Mother: "Laura, you want any more yogurt? May I have it?" Laura mumbles something, then says, "No more." Mother says, "Okay." Laura takes more things out of Mother's bag—keys, change purse, eye glasses. Laura takes the glasses out of their case. She asks Mother, "You all finished?" Mother is clearing the table and says, "I am going to have my coffee and cigarette." Laura calls out, "Look at." Mother smiles at Laura who puts Mother's glasses on.
> Laura: "You put it on me?" Mother says, "You put it on very well. They are too big for you and that is why they slip off your nose." Laura: "Look at," as she puts the glasses on again. Laura: "It is slipping down!" Mother: "Yes, I know. It is because they are too big for you, sweetheart, okay?" Laura mumbles something and Mother says, "When you are bigger." Laura: "Want one for my own." Mother says, "Yes, we will get you some sun glasses." Laura takes Mother's purse and mumbles something. She opens it and takes out some cards and scatters them around. She looks at the last one, a driver's license.
> Laura: "Mommy, that's you!" (Identifying the picture on the license.) Mother: "That's right, Laura." Laura puts it down and pulls out a dollar bill and looks at it. She gets up, then down again and takes out some coins from the change purse. She drops one, it rolls, she picks it up. She holds a handful of coins. Mother glances at Laura.

Laura takes more coins out. Laura takes out a nail file and tries to file her nails. She picks up a handful of change and stands up. She transfers all the coins to one hand. Laura walks to her room and looks at the toy shelf.

Laura looks around and babbles something, then walks to her crib and bends down to pick up a toy handbag. She unzips the bag and puts all the change in it and zips it up. She stands up and carries the toy handbag to the kitchen calling to Mother, "Look at." Mother smiles and asks, "What did you put in there?" Laura: "Money."

Laura: Excerpt 4

Laura is now twenty-seven months old and captivated by clothes.

Laura puts her feet into a play suit. She has both feet in one leg of the suit. Laura talks to herself as she tries to put on the garment. (It is a jump suit with tabs that fasten at the shoulders.) Laura pulls the suit up, talking to herself. She tries to put her hand inside the facing of one of the shoulder tabs. She says to herself, "It's wrong."

Laura struggles with the suit. She puts her hand down in one of the tabs as if thinking it's a sleeve. Laura pulls on the belt and looks down inside the suit. Laura calls to Mother, "Does it have some arms?" Mother chuckles, comes over, and buttons the suit for her. Laura: "These are overalls?" Mother: "They're culottes." Laura calls to Jennifer to look.

Jennifer ignores Laura. Mother laughs. Laura asks, "What's funny?" Mother: "You have two legs in one space, that looks funny to me." Laura looks at her knees. "I think I take this off." Mother: "Want to take it off?" She unbuttons the garment for Laura and slips it off. Laura: "Can I take off my underpants so I like to go bare naked?" Mother: "Okay—you can go bare naked. But don't leave that (culotte) lying in the middle of the floor. Put it in your crib or something." Laura: "No," but she hangs the culotte on the doorknob.

Commentary. The most obvious difference between Mrs. L and Mrs. S is that Laura's mother spends very much less time than Sonja's participating in activities with her daughter. Whereas in our observations on Sonja almost the entire time is taken up with Sonja and her mother doing something together, in Laura's case participation with her mother is an occasional thing, occurring in brief spurts as Laura herself seems to demand it. Mrs. L does converse with Laura (though much less frequently than Mrs. S), she does occasionally teach her (as in excerpt 4 when she supplies the label "culottes"), but she never takes the role of entertainer or playmate. While she nearly always encourages Laura's intellectual activities, she seldom fully throws herself into them. She is much more aloof and "adult" in her behavior.

In summary, we might say that the roles Mrs. L plays most effectively are not so much those of the participator but rather those of designer and consultant. In her role of designer she provides an environment full of interesting objects for Laura to manipulate, experiment with, operate, try on (vacuum cleaner, pot lids, handbag, shoes, clothes); others for her to look at, ponder, and interpret (television, sheafs of books); others for her to practice motor skills and work off energy (a tricycle, a swing on the porch, equipment in the playground). Laura's mother sets up rules for her access to her physical environment and, like Matthew's mother of the previous case study, is quite strict about not letting Laura use certain things she considers dangerous (like climbing on chairs or using knives, for example). But within these firmly set constraints, Laura has the run of the home and there is no lack of objects for her to play with.

Mrs. L's role as designer complements her role as consultant. When Laura meets with an interesting or difficult situation, she goes to her mother for help, information, or to share her enthusiasm (as for example when she gets information from her mother about the contents of the handbag in excerpt 3 or help with putting on the culottes in excerpt 4). Although Mrs. L is usually working on some chore or pursuing her own activities when Laura comes to her, she willingly responds to Laura, adding occasionally a naturally related idea to Laura's own thoughts (as in excerpt 3 when Mother says, "You put it (eyeglasses) on very well. They are too big for you and that is why they slip off your nose," or in excerpt 4, commenting on Laura's difficulty with putting on the culottes: "You have two legs in one space, that's funny to me."). Laura's mother spends no more than a few seconds at a time deliberately teaching Laura in these observations. Most of her teaching is done casually and in response to questions posed by Laura. Similarly, Mrs. L does not usually drop what she is doing to play with Laura for any extended periods of time (with the significant exception of a full hour per day devoted to reading, which we did not observe). She responds to Laura's initiative but does not often initiate interactive play with her or sustain it for its own sake.

We have now completed our comparison of two mothers whose styles of interaction with their young daughters seem very different. Yet both children are developing exceptionally well intellectually, so far as we can tell. Our purpose in selecting these two children for comparison was to consider the range of child-rearing styles that seem compatible with excellent developmental outcomes in children. Is there some well-defined route that caregivers must follow in order to promote their child's intellectual development? Clearly not. Once certain ingredients are present—a reasonable level of interest in observing and understanding the child's activities, an adequate amount of involvement in his tasks, a not too heavy use of restriction, a loving respect for his person—individual variation in mothers' styles seems to have not much discernible effect on the child's development, at least not by the age of three. Thus, there is probably nothing much to be gained by a mother's adopting a style of interacting which does not come naturally or easily to her, assuming her behavior already reaches adequate levels of understanding, interest, and involvement. Not every parent need emulate Sonja's mother.

This much granted, we are still faced with the difficulty of defining more precisely what are "adequate" levels of these ingredients. We sought to capture them concretely in the pictures we painted of Laura's mother and of Matthew's mother. We tried to show when they were *not* reached in our characterization of Diana's mother and will give a much more clearcut example in our story of Vicky in chapter 7. But exactly where one draws the line between adequacy and inadequacy is impossible to say. The problem becomes very complicated when we consider different values that parents may have for their children's development, especially when one set of values is emphasized at the expense of another. A case in point is given in the comparison of Brenda and Cathy in the next chapter.

6

Brenda and Cathy:
A Difference in Values

Thus far we have compared the experiences and environments of pairs of children coming from similar social class and cultural backgrounds. In this chapter we undertake with some trepidation a comparison that may seem invidious—that of an upper-middle-class child, Brenda, and a working-class child, Cathy. The purpose of this comparison is to illustrate the contrasting values for child development that parents of different social classes may have and how too heavy an emphasis on one set of values may have detrimental effects on the child's overall development. Brenda's upper-middle-class home seems excellently equipped to promote her intellectual development. But even as her mother readily stimulates and responds to Brenda's intellectual needs she seems to be training her daughter to be egotistical and demanding—to make others meet her needs rather than to adapt to and satisfy the needs of others. The opposite seems true of Cathy's mother. The pressures on Cathy are to be responsible, self-controlled, and considerate of the wishes of others. But these values seem to go hand-in-hand with a lack of responsiveness to her needs for intellectual stimulation and guidance. How then shall we assess the environment of these two children? As commentators, we find ourselves unable to reach any categorical conclusion about the "goodness" of either child's environment. Although each seems to fit the child's particular family and social class circumstances, each seems limited by its one-sidedness in promoting the child's overall development and in providing a full range of options for her in the future. But these are intuitions only. We hope therefore that the reader will take these case studies in the spirit in which they are reported: as a challenge for him to work out his own interpretations and go beyond the limitations of the present research perspective to consider more fully the relationship of social class to parental child-rearing values, the relationship of child-rearing values to child development, and finally the relationship of specific forms of development to functioning in future American society.

We shall start our case studies of Brenda and Cathy by describing their intellectual development from age one to three and then their human and physical environments.

BRENDA'S INTELLECTUAL DEVELOPMENT

When we first observed Brenda at the age of twelve months, her intellectual development was only average, as indicated by the Bayley Mental Development Index of 102 and tests of receptive language and spatial abilities. Over the course of the next two years, however, Brenda's performance on all tests improved impressively, so that by the time she was three years old her test scores were among the highest of all children in the study. Specifically, at age three her Stanford-Binet I.Q. was 139, and at thirty months she ranked fourth on our spatial abilities and third on our language test.

BRENDA'S PHYSICAL ENVIRONMENT

When we first started observing Brenda, the family lived in a six-room apartment in a residential area of Greater Boston. The neighborhood included some big mansions surrounded by spacious gardens, smaller single-family houses, and oldish apartment buildings. Brenda's family lived on the first floor of an older apartment building that was beautifully situated in terms of affording Brenda a rich, pleasant, and varied environment. Immediately adjacent was a park full of trees and a rolling meadow, a rose garden, and a well-equipped modern playground; just a few blocks away was a busy commercial district, full of small stores, shoppers, and trolleys on the street. Variety was also much in evidence within Brenda's apartment. The apartment was fairly small, consisting of a bedroom for her parents and one for the two girls, a kitchen and dining area, a small living room, and a tiny den out on the porch. But Brenda was free to roam wherever she wished in the apartment as was evident from the childish clutter and masses of toys scattered about.

We visited Brenda in this location from the time she was twelve months old to when she was fifteen months. However, by the time we began our second cycle of observations when Brenda was eighteen to twenty-one months old, her family had moved to the suburbs. They now live in an extremely large, beautifully furnished house set in spacious grounds, complete with a small hill for sliding and skiing, a hammock, swings, and sandbox. Brenda shares a bedroom, playroom, and bathroom with her sister, an arrangement obviously made by choice rather than necessity. The playroom is a delightful place with a picture window in an adjoining sunporch overlooking the grounds, a playhouse, a child's kitchen area, shelves loaded with a fabulous array of small manipulable toys, books, dolls and puppets, a swing hanging from the doorway, a tiny-tot slide, and full-length mirror. In addition, Brenda has the run of the house, including two sunny sitting rooms and an enormous kitchen decorated with her sister's artwork and mobiles hanging from the ceiling. Of all the children in our study, this child must be regarded as one of the most fortunate insofar as having a varied, stimulating, and accessible physical environment is concerned.

What now of her human environment, the people with whom Brenda comes into contact?

BRENDA'S HUMAN ENVIRONMENT

At the beginning of our study, Brenda's family was classified at about the middle of our range of middle-class families. Both parents were college educated, her father had a Ph.D. and was doing post-graduate work in science, and their income was between $7,000 and $12,000 per year. However, a large financial windfall enabled the family to move into a wealthy neighborhood during the course of our study, and this family is now at the upper end of our middle-class range. The religious and ethnic background of Brenda's parents is Northern European Protestant in the case of her mother and Jewish in the case of her father, but neither parent now professes a religious faith.

The person with whom Brenda spends most of her time is her mother. Not only was Mrs. B nearly always around when we visited (except for a period of a few months when she used a regular babysitter), but she was one of the most highly interactive mothers of our research sample. Like Sonja's mother she very often dropped what she was doing to play with her daughter and, indeed, seemed to program into her daily routine large blocks of time specifically for playing with Brenda. Of course, it should be noted, Mrs. B always had household help at her command and few pressing commitments outside the home, so it did not require any very great effort for her to do this.

Partly for these reasons, Mrs. B must be characterized as a child-centered mother. She spends a great deal of time playing and talking with her daughter, facilitating her activities, arranging a stimulating environment for her, and so on. In this she reminds us of Sonja's mother, although she is relatively less directive; she is less apt to suggest or initiate activities for Brenda but equally eager to participate in them vigorously once they are underway.

There is another point on which Brenda's mother is quite unlike Sonja's and Cathy's. This has to do with her handling of Brenda's emotional outbursts. In almost every observation we find Brenda whining or having a tantrum because her mother has frustrated one of her activities. These conflicts between Brenda and her mother seem to arise because Mrs. B spends a disproportionate amount of time responding to her intellectual needs and too little time training her to be socially responsible. Like many another mother of a bright and determined toddler, Mrs. B shies away from conflict with Brenda, apparently putting the child's desires before her own—until she loses patience. Then she becomes far from adept at handling Brenda, losing her own temper and behaving in an arbitrary and inconsistent fashion.

This brings us to Brenda herself. The picture we shall see is of a child who is obviously very bright and self-directed even at age one. She is fond of small, manipulable objects that call for fine motor activity, and, to an extent unusual for her age, is often involved in little pre-scientific experiments in which she appears to be struggling to understand the laws of nature. Equally indicative of intellectual talent is her interest in expressive role-play and verbal learning. Her ability to persist in an intellectually demanding activity is outstanding and this is associated, quite predictably, with an intense dislike of being thwarted. As previously noted, in almost every observation, Brenda spends some time protesting frustrations, and she is precociously skilled at getting her own way.

It is now time to turn to our second little girl, Cathy.

CATHY'S INTELLECTUAL DEVELOPMENT

At the beginning of our observations when she was twelve months old, Cathy's intellectual development was very advanced. Her Bayley Mental Developmental Index was 134, far higher than other children in our sample, and her performance on our language and spatial abilities tests was equally precocious. Over the course of the next two years, however, Cathy's I.Q. declined relative to standardized norms from 134 on the Bayley at twelve months, to 112 at twenty-four months, to 108 on the Stanford Binet at thirty-six months. Whereas Cathy ranked first on the Bayley of all our subjects at twelve months, she ranked tenth on the same test at twenty-four months. On our tests of language and spatial abilities,

Cathy also ranked progressively lower as she grew older. On the language tests she ranked third at fifteen months, third at twenty-four months, and eighth at thirty-six months, while on the test of spatial abilities she ranked second at twelve months, sixth at twenty-four months, and ninth at thirty months.

CATHY'S PHYSICAL ENVIRONMENT

Cathy's family lives in a deteriorated, sparsely furnished seven-room house in a residential area of Greater Boston. Their house is situated on a dead-end street and is flanked by other small houses in mixed states of repair. Half a block away is a main street with somewhat more substantial houses, but the general impression is of a lower-middle-class area with families struggling to maintain a respectable appearance. The children on the block play in their small backyards and on the dead-end street in front.

Curiously, as was the case for Brenda, the family's living situation changed during the course of our study. Sometime after the end of our second series of observations on Cathy, three bedrooms and one-and-a-half baths were added to the house to alleviate the space problem. Despite these additions, Cathy still has to share a room, aptly termed a "dormitory" by the family, with four other siblings. Also, since this change did not take place till Cathy was nearly two, many of the observations to be discussed in this case study took place when living quarters for the family were extremely cramped. At that time, the house consisted of one floor with two bedrooms and the "dormitory," a bedroom in the attic and one in the cellar, a kitchen, and a living room. All the bedrooms, save the dormitory, were off limits to Cathy and she spent most of her time near the large central table in the kitchen, the television set in the living room, and the dead-end street in front of the house where the family frequently congregated for entertainment and socializing.

CATHY'S HUMAN ENVIRONMENT

In terms of income, residence, and education, Cathy's family must be classified at the lower end of the range of working-class families in our study. Her father works at a semiskilled building maintenance job, and their income, for a family of fifteen people, is about $8,000 per year. Neither parent has more than a high school education, but their oldest child is now attending a state college, and Mrs. C has also recently started art lessons. The parents and children are all Catholics and their ethnic background Southern European. The people with whom Cathy spends most time are her siblings, particularly her four-year-old sister, a teenage sister, and a pre-teenage brother under whose supervision she is frequently left, as her mother busies herself with the household chores. During all our observations, Cathy was nominally in her mother's charge, but with brothers and sisters very often around more than half of her interaction took place with them.

The picture we get of Mrs. C is of a mother who has changed very little her style of interacting with her daughter during a period of her child's life when development is extremely rapid. Whether Cathy was twelve months old or thirty months old, Mrs. C finds very little time to engage with her in activities that are intellectually stimulating. Clearly, a major reason for this is that with a large family to look after, Mrs. C is a very busy woman and it is a rare occasion that she literally has the time to devote undivided attention to any one child. This situation would not be detrimental if Cathy got the intellectual stimulation she needs from her brothers and sisters. However, our observations show that Cathy engages in few intellectually stimulating activities with her siblings and apparently they never try to teach her.

On the other hand, we should note that a truly outstanding feature about Mrs. C's home is the atmosphere of cheerfulness, harmony, and smooth social relationships. Mrs. C seldom raises her voice at the children, manages the home with efficiency, and demonstrates much love, good humor, and patience toward her family. Cathy's mother must be characterized as positive, loving, and encouraging towards her, but her daughter's intellectual development is not one of her primary concerns.

OBSERVATIONS ON BRENDA AND CATHY

We shall start with two observations made when Brenda and Cathy were approximately twelve months old.

Brenda: Excerpt 1

The scene opens with Brenda and her mother sitting on the kitchen floor playing with that universally appealing plaything of a one-year-old—the kitchen pots and pans.

> Mother gets a tea kettle and hands it to Brenda. Brenda puts the lid on. Mother says, "Yeah, yeah." Brenda smiles at Mother. She puts the lid on again. Mother claps her hands and smiles. Brenda takes it off and puts it on again, and smiles proudly to Mother. Mother smiles back. Brenda looks at the observer then at Mother and puts the lid on and off.

Brenda smiles and puts the lid on again. She tries to take the lid off, saying, "Oh-oh." Mother says, "You can get it off." Brenda takes it off and picks up another lid with her other hand. Mother looks on. Brenda takes the tea kettle lid off and shows it to Mother. Mother says, "Yes, you got it." Brenda puts it back on the kettle and babbles. She makes an "oh-oh" sound and waves to Mother. Mother waves back. Brenda plays with the lid.

Brenda looks at the observer and makes an "oh-oh" sound. She tries to put the lid on, then takes it off and shows it to Mother. Mother says, "You got it again." Brenda sits down on the floor, puts the lid on the chair, then puts the lid on the tea kettle, then pulls herself up again, babbling.

Brenda picks up the other lid and tries to put it on the tea kettle. Mother gets up and goes out to the children's room. Mother comes back and hands a toy pot to Brenda saying, "Here, dear." Brenda handles it and Mother sits down again, looking at her as she puts the other lid on the pot. Mother says, "Yes." Brenda bangs the lid on the toy pot, then bangs it on the chair, then on the pot again. She bangs the lid on the chair then on the pot again. She continues banging.

Brenda picks up the tea kettle lid. Mother smiles as she looks on. Brenda puts the lid in her mouth and makes a vocal sound. Mother gets up and walks by her, patting her head gently and saying, "You play here." Mother walks to her room.

Cathy: Excerpt 1

The excerpt begins with Cathy crawling around the kitchen floor. Five brothers and sisters are in the vicinity and her mother is busy cleaning up.

Cathy smiles at the observer then crawls around the kitchen while Mother talks to a sibling. Cathy touches the refrigerator, plug, handles cord of the telephone, then pokes her finger into the phone dial. She walks to the children's bedroom, then to the bed. A sister is in the room. Cathy leans down to look under the bed, hits her face, and whimpers.

Cathy plays with a towel, turning it over and waving it about. She puts the towel to her mouth, then goes to a chest of drawers and gets another towel.

Cathy puts her head on the bed. Mother comes into the bedroom, smiles at her and Cathy smiles back. Mother leaves. Cathy stands with the towel in her mouth. She pulls the towel between the crib bars, pulls it out again, then drops it. Cathy babbles to her sister who tells her to come on. Cathy walks into the open closet.

Cathy's sister watches Cathy in the closet, then runs away. Cathy stays in the closet looking at the observer. Her sister tries to pull Cathy out but she resists, pulling back. Her sister pats Cathy's head and leaves. Cathy stays in the closet.

Cathy stays in the closet, sitting down and looking around. Cathy touches a shoe, turning it around and looking at it. Cathy stares at the observer. She stays in the closet, pulling at a laundry box.

Commentary. The contrast between these two excerpts is dramatic. For the entire five minutes of observation, Brenda is involved in an intellectually valuable activity, as she learns the spatial concepts and fine motor coordination necessary to fit a lid on a pot. Cathy, on the other hand, spends an equivalent amount of time in unsystematic exploration with objects she happens to come across. Of course, much of Cathy's behavior may be ascribed to the newness of the situation of being observed (although the situation is equally unfamiliar to Brenda) but, as we shall see, the contrast between the two children's behavior is not unique to this initial observation but holds through many subsequent visits.

The striking difference in the behavior of the children's mothers is equally indicative. Brenda's mother spends almost the entire five minutes facilitating her activity: she supplies pots and pans when needed, she encourages her when she falters, she praises her when she fits the lid on, she carefully observes her attempts at mastery. In contrast, Cathy's mother spends exactly five seconds interacting with her—the time it takes to smile lovingly at a child and receive a smile in return. These two exceedingly brief excerpts contain in microcosm the contrast in the environments of Brenda and Cathy that the remaining excerpts will amplify.

In the next observation Brenda is about thirteen-and-a-half months old. It is lunch time and she has been cranky, presumably because Mother was late coming home and she is hungry. Mother, too, is not at her best, having just tried to deal unsuccessfully with one of Brenda's tantrums. The scene opens with Mother at the door welcoming home Brenda's sister, while Brenda sits in her highchair at the kitchen table. Brenda, on her own and quieting down after her tantrum, launches into one of her little "scientific" experiments: her topic, the law of floating bodies.

Brenda: Excerpt 2

Brenda pushes her glass of milk away, sliding it along the table top. Suddenly she drops a piece of meat into the glass and it sinks. She startles slightly and then deliberately puts a potato chip in and it floats. She looks puzzled.

Brenda puts her hand deep into the glass and seems to be searching for the piece of meat at the bottom. She lifts the glass toward her, peers into it, then pushes it away. Brenda puts her hand in again and waves her fingers about in the milk several times as if trying to reach the meat. Mother comes in with her sister, Jennifer. Mother, "Pretty good! (referring to the fact that Brenda had eaten some food) Do you want a drink?"

Mother holds the glass of milk for Brenda and she drinks. As Mother begins to take away the glass, Brenda starts to screech. Mother: "Oh, you are naughty today!" and goes to the kitchen leaving the glass on the table. Brenda slides the glass over and drops a chip in, resuming her experiment. Mother returns, removes the glass well out of Brenda's reach, lifts her out of the chair, sits her on the floor, and leaves. Brenda starts screaming and whimpering.

Mother comes in and wipes the table, deliberately ignoring Brenda's tantrum that continues for four more minutes.

Cathy: Excerpt 2

Cathy falls at the doorway to the living room, picks herself up and cries. Mother turns around and asks, "What's the matter? What happened?" Cathy walks to Mother. "Did you fall?" Mother bends down to hug Cathy, saying, "Okay, okay. You want the kleenex?" Mother hands Cathy a wet paper towel. Cathy takes it and starts to wipe the kitchen table. Mother looks on and says, "Clean, clean." Mother goes back to work at the sink. Cathy walks around the table, wiping it with short motions. Cathy takes the wet towel to the living room and goes to clean the chair, then the cabinet.

Cathy cleans the couch with the wet towel, then the chair on which a brother is sitting watching Sesame Street. Cathy goes to a sister, wipes her chair, then wipes the couch again. Cathy walks to the kitchen, wipes the high-chair near the doorway, then the ice box. Mother leaves then comes back in.

Mother looks at Cathy, repeating, **"Clean, clean, clean!"** and walks to the hall. Cathy walks around, wiping the stove, then the ice box again, then the T.V. screen in the living room. Cathy wipes the chest of drawers, the window sill, the chair. (Cathy continues wiping and cleaning until the end of the observation.)

Commentary.   Brenda's activities and Cathy's activities in these two excerpts are similar in that they are to a large extent self-initiated and self-directed with minimal input from other people. We see both children here involved in intellectually valuable activities. Brenda is grappling to understand the laws of flotation, Cathy to master a sequence of "executive skills" as she wipes the furniture, imitating, no doubt, what she has often seen her mother do. The behavior of Brenda's mother here compares unfavorably with that of Cathy's mother. Mrs. B inadvertently cuts short Brenda's scientific experiment thereby provoking a tantrum, and is unable to change Brenda's emotional response. Mrs. B's less than adept handling of Brenda's emotional behavior seems characteristic of her. As we stated before, in almost all of our observations Brenda spends some time whining or protesting and her mother seems not to have developed appropriate techniques of dealing with her outbursts. Brenda's mother is much more skillful at interacting with her daughter in the context of activities where she can use a nicely balanced mixture of techniques of teaching, participation, facilitation, and observation to promote clear-cut intellectual goals.

Cathy's excerpt shows Mrs. C in a characteristic light. She is ready to comfort Cathy when she falls, and adept at distracting her from her preoccupation with her hurt to a constructive activity. Even with regard to intellectual stimulation Mrs. C's behavior seems well enough adapted to Cathy's activity. She lets her get on with the task of learning, yet helps to sustain her interest by appropriate words of encouragement and praise, as she busies herself with household chores similar to those Cathy is undertaking. The problem for Cathy is that she experiences *so few* interactions of this type and when they come they are so fleeting. More

typical of the contrast in the experiences of Brenda and Cathy are the
events described below.

Brenda: Excerpt 3

This excerpt comes from an observation made when Brenda was close
to nineteen months old. As usual, Brenda has just had a small tantrum
because her mother stopped her from playing with a chain of safety pins
that she had found. Mother now takes her into the playroom and distracts
her with a safe substitute—a toy necklace and a barrette that Mrs. B
pins in Brenda's hair. This distraction, presumably intended by her mother
to initiate a dress-up sequence, turns into another of the little "scientific"
experiments which this little girl loves. Her topics this time are "reflection"
and "gravity."

> Mother clips a small barrette on Brenda's hair. Mother: "You can see it in
> the mirror." (There is a full-length mirror on the wall a few feet away.) Brenda
> looks around, puzzled. Mother repeats, "Look in the mirror!" Brenda moves
> toward the mirror and Mother points to the barrette in her hair, as Brenda
> looks in the mirror. Mother: "You have to get near to see it," and leads her
> nearer to the mirror. Mother: "See your barrette? See it?" Brenda pulls at
> her hair and at the clip. She still seems puzzled. It seems as if she can't
> reconcile the feel of the barrette in one location (her hair that her hand is
> touching), and seeing it in front of her in another position. Mother fixes the
> barrette in her hair and says, "You are not watching. Look there!" Mother
> points to the reflection in the mirror, and Brenda stares still pulling at her
> hair, with a puzzled expression. Mother asks Brenda's one-year-old playmate,
> Tom, if he wants a barrette, too.
>
> Brenda holds out her hand, gesturing for the can full of barrettes and
> little ornaments that her Mother has taken down. Mother gives her the can
> and Brenda takes out a barrette. Brenda takes the barrette to Tom and tries
> to clip it in his hair. Not knowing how to do this, she simply places it on his
> hair and it falls. Mother observes, and says, "Here's a nice one to put in his
> hair." Mother slowly clips one in the boy's hair, demonstrating to Brenda how
> it works. Brenda looks on. Mother leaves the room.
>
> Brenda tries to clip the barrette on Tom's hair, moving the clip a little,
> but again it falls off. Brenda puts several clips back into the can, one by one.
> She puts the cover on the can and screws it slightly. She takes off the neck-
> lace from around her neck. Brenda puts a barrette on her hair, again not
> clipping it but placing it on her hair, and it falls off.
>
> She repeats this action two or three times. She turns her attention to taking
> the small barrettes and ornaments one by one from the can and putting them
> back in, examining each carefully, apparently still trying to understand how
> their clips work. Brenda covers the can and screws on the top. (She continues
> with her exploration for several minutes after the end of this observation.)

Cathy: Excerpt 3

The next excerpt from Cathy's observations provides a sharp contrast to
Brenda's excerpt 3. Both observations were done when the children were

eighteen to nineteen months old. In this excerpt, Cathy has found a paper bag full of sea shells that her brother has collected and is playing with them in the kitchen.

Cathy takes the shells out of the bag one by one, putting them on the floor. Cathy places the shells one by one on the seat of a chair next to her. She stacks one shell on another like two saucers.

She continues placing the shells on the chair, putting them on the floor, then putting them on the chair again. She handles the shells one by one.

She stacks about six or seven shells, one by one, on the floor. Mother returns to the kitchen. Cathy holds out the stack of shells to her mother (holding the stack by the bottom shell quite carefully). Mother says, "Put them back, quick! Put the rest back in. You got one on the floor." Mother goes to the stove. Cathy puts a handful of shells (from the stack which has now disintegrated) into the bag.

Cathy puts a few more shells into the bag, one by one, and squeezes together the mouth of the bag. She looks around the floor, obviously searching to see if any are left. She gets up holding the bag and walks to Mother. Mother: "Have you got them all?" Mother glances around at the floor, satisfying herself that there are no shells remaining there.

Commentary.   Brenda's excerpt is remarkable again for the topic of the child's interest, and also for the length of time she persists at the task of understanding first how an object in one place can be reflected in another, and second, how mechanisms operate to keep things from falling. In this episode, her mother takes a more assertive and directive approach, not succeeding particularly well, because the child does not seem to learn much about reflection or how to operate the clip from her mother's efforts. Nevertheless, by supplying the materials for the experiment (mirror and barrette) and showing enthusiastic interest, Brenda's mother has at least posed the question for Brenda, who continues to grapple with it long after the mother quits the scene.

Perhaps the major point of contrast between the excerpts from Brenda and Cathy is in the mother's awareness of what the activity in question means to the child, what she might be learning from it. Brenda's mother makes a deliberate attempt to teach Brenda the concept of "reflection" with the mirror and is not conspicuously successful in doing so. But she poses the problem for Brenda, thereby setting off a train of exploration that, in a child as bright as Brenda, will very likely culminate soon in a rudimentary understanding of the concept. In contrast, Cathy's mother seems unaware of the intellectual significance of Cathy's stacking the shells. We view this as an intellectually valuable activity that provides an opportunity for the child to learn spatial relationships; but, clearly, Mrs. C is only concerned with the housekeeping aspect—that the child should not clutter the floor or damage her brother's possessions. In a large family with little space, it is probably necessary to enforce rules of possession, but a price is paid, unwittingly, as this excerpt illustrates.

Brenda: Excerpt 4

The fourth excerpt comes from an observation when Brenda was twenty-one months old. It provides a beautiful example of an intellectually valuable activity involving verbal learning for Brenda and a mixture of direct teaching and active participation on the part of her mother and sister. It is again remarkable for the length of time that Brenda sustains interest in the task and for the mother's enthusiastic, highly participatory approach.

> Brenda takes out a plastic animal from a box and makes a noise. Mother says, "Neigh, neigh—that's a horse." Brenda: "Horse." Mother looks on as Brenda labels and makes a "moo" noise. Brenda drops the horse on the table and tries to reach for Mother's address file. Mother: "No, no, you can't play with Mommy's card. Find more animals. Find a cow." Brenda looks through the box.
>
> Brenda takes out another animal and makes a "moo-moo" sound. Mother: "You found it!" Brenda: "Moo." Mother: "Moo." They laugh. Mother and Brenda's sister Rachel label for Brenda: "Cow." Mother: "Can you stand it up?" Brenda makes the cow stand up. Mother suggests Brenda go find more animals. Brenda goes back to the box. She takes out another one and says, "Neigh, neigh." Mother: "Yes, that's another horse."
>
> Rachel says, "Black one." Mother: "Yes, that's a big black one." Brenda: "Black." Mother: "Yes, black horse." Mother suggests a dog. Brenda: "No," but she goes to find it. Mother: "No doggie? Look some more." Rachel offers to help. Brenda looks on, as Rachel rummages through the box. Brenda glances at the rain and snow outside. Rachel hands Brenda another cow. Brenda looks at it. Brenda stands it on the table and says, "Moo."
>
> Brenda looks on and waits. Mother helps to look for the dog. Mother shows Brenda another animal. "What's that, Brenda?" Brenda: "Mew, mew." Mother: "What does a dog say?" Rachel: "That's a dog." Mother: "Yes." Brenda looks on as Mother rummages and takes out another animal and makes a roaring noise. Brenda: "Lion!" Mother: "That's right. That's a lion."
>
> Mother: "Here's another one," and puts a calf on the table. Brenda looks on and then says: "Moo-moo." Mother smiles as Brenda says, "Moo-cow, moo-cow!" in excitement. Brenda looks at the lion and makes a roaring noise. Mother looks through the box and takes out another animal. Brenda makes a "baa-baa" noise at the lamb. Mother looks on as Brenda says, "Baa," then makes a roaring noise at the lion. Mother: "That's a lion," and makes a roaring noise also. Brenda joins in. Mother: "That's right." Brenda makes a "baa" noise. Mother: "Which one says baa?" Brenda looks. Mother: "This one!" and points. Mother and Brenda make "baa" noises. Brenda picks up the lamb, as Mother looks on.

Cathy: Excerpt 4

Cathy's excerpt comes from an observation when she was twenty-one months old. The activities described in both Brenda's and Cathy's excerpts

deal with the learning of names for things. Cathy's mother is more attentive to Cathy than is typical for her, yet there is a considerable contrast
between her and Mrs. B in both the quantity and quality of interaction
with their daughters.

Mother has been feeding Cathy a bowl of noodles and prepares to clean up
Cathy's messy face and hands.

Mother: "How about your face?" Mother wipes Cathy's hands with a wet
towel. Cathy says something. Mother: "You want to hold it?" Mother gives
Cathy the folded wet towel. Mother: "Wipe your face." Cathy takes the towel
and rubs her mouth. She opens up the towel and puts it on the tray. Cathy:
"Clean." Mother: "That's right, clean." Cathy: "Fold it," as she rolls the
towel up, putting one end over toward the middle and pushing at the bulky
end. Mother: "Fold it." Mother goes back to the sink and starts doing the
dishes. Cathy straightens out the towel on the tray by pulling at the edge
nearest her, then crumples it up, squeezing it in the middle.

Cathy wipes her mouth with the towel. She babbles as she hangs the
towel over the side of the highchair, holding it by one end. Mother: "Wait
a minute." (Apparently thinking Cathy wants to get out of the chair.) Cathy
puts the towel over her face. Mother: "Do you want to get down?" Cathy
says nothing and Mother lifts her out. Cathy: "Water." Mother: "Do you want
water on this (the towel) to get it clean?" Mother gives Cathy the wet towel
(without wetting it any more), saying, "What are you going to clean?" Cathy:
"Face." Mother: "You are going to clean up your face?" Cathy puts the
towel over her face. Mother watches her. Cathy: "Wash face." Mother: "You
are washing your face." Mother goes back to the sink. Cathy wipes the table
with the towel, then her cheek. Cathy blows her nose in the towel, and follows
Mother to the door in the kitchen that opens to the backyard.

Commentary.   Cathy's mother is usually at her best (so far as promoting Cathy's intellectual development) when she is interacting with
Cathy in the context of some household chore or basic care activity—in
this example, cleaning her up after a meal. It is on these occasions that
Mrs. C usually finds the time to instruct Cathy either in attaining some
practical skill or in the names for things, and Mrs. C does both things in
this example. Nevertheless, Mrs. B's interaction may be contrasted with
that of Mrs. C in the length of time she engages in teaching Brenda and
the quality of excitement involved, as she dramatizes the animal sounds.
It is true that Mrs. C provides feedback to Cathy that her labels are
correct ("clean," "fold it," and in: Cathy: "Wash face." Mother: "You
are washing your face.") but the teaching aspect simply does not go
very far. Mrs. C could have extended Cathy's budding interest in language
by making a game out of washing different parts of the body or by elaborating her labels in a number of realistic ways. Instead she leaves the
initiative entirely to Cathy and responds to her cues only in a rather
limited way.

Brenda: Excerpt 5

In this excerpt Brenda's mother again uses a characteristic approach—a mixture of participation, direction, encouragement, praise, and observation of the child's attempts to master a difficult skill. The scene opens with Brenda, age thirty months, Mother, and Rachel watering plants in the garden.

Brenda waters a plant as Mother watches. Brenda looks into the watering can. Mother: "Oh, that's too much water. You'll drown it!" Brenda watches as Mother redistributes water in the pot. Mother suggests they get some more water because all the plants have not been watered. Brenda picks up some flowers she had cut. Mother observes her.

Brenda tells her sister, "This is mine." (Referring to the flowers.) She carries the watering can to the house saying to herself, ". . . get more water." She walks with Mother who says, "I'll get you a vase for the flowers." Brenda repeats, "Get me a vase and put this in a can." Brenda follows Mother into the kitchen. Father asks where Brenda got the flowers. She holds them out to Father, for him to see.

She tells Father, "We get some water," and Father nods. She asks for water. Mother shows her a glass vase for the flowers. Mother suggests Brenda put some water in the vase. Brenda fills the vase with water from the watering can. Mother tells Brenda that the dog found the bone she left for him. Brenda carries the vase to the table and puts the flowers in carefully one by one.

Brenda continues putting the flowers in the vase. She calls, "I put them both in." Mother suggests that she wipe off the bottom of the vase. Brenda tells Mother, "I'll put them right there." Mother asks, "On the table? Or in the living room? I don't care."

Brenda: "Yeah, in the living room." Mother suggests she take the flowers to the living room and.put them on "whatever table you want." Brenda carries the vase through the hall to the living room. Brenda sets the vase on the table. She says to herself, "Nobody can't get it." She picks up the flower shears, opens and closes them with both hands. She continues.

Brenda goes near the record player and listens to "Yellow Submarine." Brenda listens. Brenda walks away from the record player. She picks up the flower shears and opens and closes them. Mother suggests Brenda cut off the dead flowers from among those arranged in the vase.

Brenda asks: "Which ones are dead?" Mother shows her a few brown flowers. Brenda says she wants to water the flowers. Mother: "Okay, but we'll have to cut them off."

Cathy: Excerpt 5

This observation was made when Cathy was thirty-two months old. We could not resist comparing it with Brenda's flower-arranging efforts because Cathy, too, starts off by being excited by the smell and feel of growing things, although her experience ends on quite a different note.

Cathy pulls off a leaf from a bush. She smells it and in great excitement runs to her sister, Mary, saying, "Smell that," pushing the leaf under her sister's nose. Mary smiles approvingly.

Cathy gets more leaves and takes them to Mary again. Mary smells then pushes her away playfully. Cathy watches Mary strip off leaves. Mary: "Want to smell my flower?" Cathy smiles and buries her nose in Mary's leaves. She runs back to the fence, shouting to Mary, "Want to smell mine?" She takes some leaves to Mary. Mary pushes the leaves in Cathy's face. "Smell one."

Cathy looks around on the ground, singing to herself. Mary moves off. Cathy strips off a handful of leaves and smiles to herself. Mary comes over with plastic sand toys. Cathy: "Smell my flower?" Mary pushes her away uninterested. "I'm making supper." Cathy watches Mary pour dirt from one container to another. Cathy studies the leaves, turning them all around, brushing them with her hand.

Cathy watches Mary pouring sand. Cathy pushes leaves in Mary's face. Mary pushes Cathy away firmly. Cathy puts a handful of dirt on her leg, lifts her pants leg, rubs dirt on her leg, and pulls down the pants leg. She repeats this with her other leg. Cathy lifts up her pants leg and looks at the dirt on her leg. She puts on her sock

Cathy continues pulling up her sock. She rubs her leg, as if wiping off the dirt. She pulls her pants legs over her knees. She scoops up some dirt in a plastic container. Cathy scoops more dirt into the plastic container, imitating her sister, but not interacting with her.

Commentary. In reading Brenda's excerpt the reader should not forget that she is only thirty months old. Not every mother encourages her two-and-a-half-year old to handle breakable vases or dangerous shears! Although this particular liberty need not be advocated, the episode illustrates a point that is generally true of middle-class mothers of well-developing children: they permit their children to engage in activities that other mothers more often prohibit—activities that are somewhat dangerous, somewhat inconvenient, and somewhat beyond the abilities of a child so young. Their encouragement of these activities may spring from a detailed knowledge of their own child's skills, interest, and character, from an appreciation of the significance of such activities to the child's intellectual development, or simply because they enjoy playing with children. Many mothers who seem so adept at shaping their children's intellectual development apparently have no conscious intention of doing so—at least not when they undertake any specific activity. They engage in these activities just because they are an interesting way to pass time with their children, and their interactions are not necessarily deliberate or planned in advance.

Cathy's excerpt illustrates a different point, namely, that although a sibling who is fairly close in age to a younger one may be an effective mother surrogate (as was the case with Matthew's and Diana's brothers of chapter 4), that is not always true. A child of four or five is still largely egocentric and tends to use a younger sibling as an adjunct to his activity rather than as a true participant. His own selfish needs often conflict with those of his younger sibling and, unlike an adult, the preschool child does not participate in activities for the sake of his younger sibling. Thus, although excerpt 5 begins delightfully as Cathy and her sister excitedly smell the freshly cut leaves, Mary quickly tires of Cathy's childish glee and pushes her away to begin her own supper-from-dirt preparations. Cathy's imitation of Mary's actions, pouring dirt from one container to the other, poignantly suggests how much she would like to be included in her sister's make-believe world; but Mary will have none of it and Cathy has to shift for herself.

Our final excerpts illustrate the central point that we made in the introduction to these two case studies. We noted there that Brenda's home was excellently geared to promote her intellectual development, Cathy's to foster her social development. In terms of the physical environment—the places and playthings available to the child—there is an immense difference between Brenda's home and that of Cathy. Brenda is among the most fortunate of our subjects in the rich store of well-designed toys she possesses and in her freedom to wander about anywhere in her family's large, well-furnished house, exploring household objects almost at will. Cathy, in comparison, has fewer than the average number of toys (even for children of the same social class in our study), and many of the toys she plays with belong to her brothers and sisters and are subject to removal by rule or by whim. There is probably no simple, straightforward relationship between the abundance of the child's physical environment and his development, intellectual or social. A child who is "given every-thing" may be no better off than the child who has to make something out of nothing. Some balance between overabundance and total deprivation seems best, but it is hard to say where this balance should be struck.

A difficulty arises for us in this study in that our observational scales are heavily biased toward seeing the value of an experience for the child's intellectual development rather than his social development. Unless the social relevance of a child's experience is very salient, we tend to evaluate each episode strictly according to the opportunity it presents for promoting the child's intellectual growth. Yet, it often happens that the same experience—for example Cathy's mother's restricting Cathy's highly intellectual activity with the seashells in excerpt 3—may be seen as detrimental to the child's intellectual development but beneficial to his social development. With a large family cramped for space, Cathy has to learn not to interfere with her siblings' prized possessions and to keep out of their territory, so to speak. She also has to learn to respect her mother's authority and to obey promptly. With thirteen children to attend to, her mother cannot afford to be inconsistent or to engage in long explanations about why certain things have to be done. Mrs. C believes that she should put few restrictions on Cathy's activities, but that when restriction is necessary it should be enforced, and that Cathy must learn that whining and crying will not get her her way.

By comparison, Brenda's mother is much more likely to succumb to Brenda's protests at being restricted. Either she gives in and lets Brenda have her own way, or else she uses the technique of distracting the child to another interesting intellectually valuable activity. Either way, from the point of view of our research, a mother like Mrs. B seems to be promoting her child's intellectual development, while a mother like Mrs. C seems to be curtailing it. But the same experiences viewed from the perspective of the child's social-emotional development, may place these two mothers in a different light. Cathy's mother may then be seen as teaching the child what she needs to learn to develop as a social being responsive to the needs of others, whereas Brenda's mother seems to be teaching her how to make others satisfy *her own* needs. It does not escape us as observers that many middle-class mothers inculcate early a sense of "me first" in their children, while working-class parents more often instill the notion of "others first." This contrast is evident in our final set of excerpts.

Brenda: Excerpt 6

We shall give two excerpts from our observations on Brenda to illustrate her mother's two characteristic responses to her whining and fussing. In the first excerpt Brenda is just nineteen months old. We come upon her exploring the contents of an inlaid cabinet in the sunroom.

> Brenda finds a string of small safety pins in a tiny drawer. She pulls the string out of the drawer, tosses it on the floor, picks it up again, and stretches it taut across her chest. Brenda rolls the string up in a ball, stretches it out, then winds it up again. Her mother comes in and sees her. Mother: "Put it back," and opens the drawer. Brenda drops the string in without protest but holds on to the drawer, babbling to Mother. (She apparently wants something else in the drawer.)
>
> Mother: "No, shut the drawer," Brenda begins to squeal, pushing against Mother to get at the drawer. Brenda shrieks in anger. Mother: "No, we'll get you something else to play with." Mother lifts Brenda up and carries her upstairs. Brenda continues crying. Mother takes her into the playroom and gives her a long necklace from her toy trinket-box, then a barrette for her hair. (The excerpt continues with the "barrette" episode described in excerpt 3.)

Brenda: Excerpt 7

Brenda, age twenty-seven months, is in the backyard. She has discovered the hose that is filling the children's wading pool and is experimenting with spraying the water in different directions. Her sister, Rachel, age five years, comes over and tells Brenda not to play with the hose.

Brenda shouts, "I make the water go!" Rachel goes to the faucet to turn it off and Brenda yells, "Don't do that!" Rachel turns the faucet the wrong way and the water comes out even faster. Mother shouts from around the corner of the house, "Brenda, no! Not that way!" (Apparently thinking it was Brenda who turned the faucet on.)

Brenda starts screaming and throws the hose down in anger. Mother comes over, talks to Rachel, and turns the faucet off. Brenda runs over whining, "I want more water!" Mother ignores Brenda and continues talking to Rachel. Brenda yells several times, "I want more water!" and begins to scream. Mother shrieks, "Okay, no more, no more!" Then, as Brenda continues screaming, says in a softer voice, "Okay, you can have some over here," and begins to move the hose to a different spot for Brenda to use.

Brenda yells, "No!" and continues screaming. Mother shrugs, turns on the faucet and says, in a conciliatory tone, "Do you want to water the flowers? Here you are." She gives Brenda the hose and Brenda pulls it back toward her original spot near the pool. Mother walks away. (Brenda resumes her experiment with the hose, continuing until the end of the observation.)

Commentary.   In both excerpts we find Brenda pursuing an "intellectual" activity that her mother interrupts. Her mother's response to her anger at being frustrated is to distract her to another "intellectual" activity in the first excerpt and to let her have her own way in the second. This type of interaction—anger-distraction or anger-yielding—occurred many times in our observations of Brenda and her mother. In contrast, we seldom saw Cathy sulk, whine, or have a tantrum, and when she did this was how her mother responded:

Cathy: Excerpt 6

Cathy, thirty-three months, looks on as Mother puts mittens on her sister, Sharon. Cathy looks around, then goes to the coat hooks. "They are mine." Mary, another sister, hands Cathy the pair of red mittens that Mother has just handed to her, but Mother stops her and starts to put them on Mary. Cathy whines. Mother: "They are too big for you." Cathy cries. Mother ignores.

Cathy whines and looks on as Mother attends to Mary. Cathy cries and follows them to Mother's room, then out to the kitchen again. Mother: "Come here, Cathy." Cathy follows Mother on down to the hall, still crying. Cathy follows Mother into Cathy's room whining, "Mary, Mary." Mother says, "Mary hasn't got yours. They aren't yours," and takes Cathy's hand and leads her into the boys' room. Cathy cries. Mother picks up a pair of smaller red mittens off the bed and says, "See, these are yours. You want to put them on?" Cathy cries, "No." Mother: "Okay, you don't want them?" Mother takes the mittens and leads Cathy by the hand to the kitchen. Mother puts the mittens on the kitchen table and goes to attend to her laundry. Cathy cries. She looks on as Mother attends to Sharon and cries, "Mary." Mary hands Cathy the mittens from the table. Cathy doesn't want them and cries, "Give me." (Wanting Mary's mittens.) Mary starts to give her the mittens but Mother says, "Don't give them to her. They're not hers."

Cathy starts to cry. Mary looks on. Mother repeats to Mary, "Don't give them to her," then to Cathy, "They are not yours." Cathy continues crying. She goes out to the hall, following her sisters who are ready to go play outside, still crying. Mother: "Come here." Mother and Cathy go to the kitchen table and Mother picks up Cathy's red mittens and says, "These are yours, you want them on?" Cathy shakes her head and cries, "No, I want Mary's." Mother says firmly, "No, Mary didn't have yours." Cathy cries and looks on as Mother talks to a brother. Cathy continues crying to the end of the observation.

Commentary. Mrs. C's behavior in this excerpt reminds us very much of Matthew's mother's handling of his tantrum when she refused to let him play with his milk and gave it to his brother. She seems to teach Cathy a lesson in social responsibility (she may not have what does not belong to her) and does so firmly and with composure, despite the ubiquitous presence of an observer recording her daughter's acting up. Mrs. C does not succumb to Cathy's tears and temper. She explains why she may not have her sister's mittens, offers her a fair alternative, and if Cathy still wants to sulk or cry, so be it. Unlike Brenda's mother, Mrs. C does not give in to Cathy's whims however intellectually-inspired these might be. She will not run the risk of spoiling Cathy. This point of view is elaborated in Mrs. C's own words in our final interview with her.

INTERVIEW WITH MRS. C

Asked about Cathy's personality and socio-emotional development, her mother described Cathy as outgoing, independent, easygoing, cooperative, and compliant. Generally, she gave very little trouble, but compared to her older brothers and sisters, she was becoming a little "spoilt" and this tendency had to be nipped in the bud.

"I never had any trouble with the other kids when it was a birthday, and they got a gift. It was their birthday, and that's it. But once in a while, Cathy'll say, 'How come I don't get something? I want a doll like she's got!' And I'll say, 'It's not your birthday, and you can't have it.' She'll kind of moan and groan for a while, then she'll get over it. But, it's not a serious thing. *She's got to learn not to expect too much.*"

The words, "She's got to learn not to expect too much," summarize in a nutshell Mrs. C's attitude toward providing intellectually stimulating playthings for Cathy. Hers is not a thoughtless position. She has good reasons for it, and she offers them honestly, as in the following:

"I don't believe in these expensive toys because I think they just see them on T.V. It seems wonderful on T.V., but when they get them home, they aren't wonderful at all. The kids aren't even looking for real expensive toys. Because when you buy them one, they'll put it aside and play with little things that don't amount to much. And I think they learn more. Like if you get a little puzzle—they don't cost too much—they'll spend hours on it. Now, take a tiny baby—they have so many toys for them in the stores, and what do they like to play with? Pots and pans."

Similarly, Mrs. C has sound reasons for making strict rules about Cathy's playing with certain toys and possessions belonging to others— her sisters' books, her brothers' cars, her mother's dressing-table ornaments. The family cannot easily afford to replace articles broken in a toddler's curious explorations:

"There are certain things I won't let her play with. On my table I have a couple of little china animals that I don't want her to touch or break because they mean so much to me. If I'm in there, then I tell her she can play with them right there and she will. She can't take them out of the room or she will be punished for it. Make no mistake."

Mrs C's attitude toward providing intellectual stimulation for Cathy goes beyond the question of playthings. She believes (again, with justification, given her onerous family responsibilities), that she cannot afford to pay too much attention to Cathy and allow her to become dependent on such attention. Thus, when asked whether it was important to teach a young child specific skills or give information, Mrs. C relates the question to a problem that is important to her and candidly replies:

"Take religion now. They want the parents to teach the catechism and so on, because there aren't enough nuns to do it. I said, as far as teaching, I'm no good as a teacher. But as far as religion, the way I live is the best way to teach them. The way you live, the kids fall right into it— because if you live a good life, they'll try to follow the same way. So I try to spend what time I can with her. I'm against the idea that all you have to do is to sit down and read or do things with them. I have to do my work around . . . and really, there is more work to do than anything else. I mean, you just don't have the time to spend like that, with a family big like mine."

What, then, were the most important things to stress in bringing up a young child? Mrs. C:

"I think that the most important thing is discipline and love. Give him enough love and discipline and I think they'll have security. Today, it's 'do your own thing.' I don't think that a kid really knows what they are doing when they're so young. And they won't do anything if you're always asking yes or no, and it's up to them. Certain things, they just have to follow. You've got to look down the line and say, 'This is your job, this is yours, and this is yours,' and they've got to do it. And if they don't, they get punished for it.

"Talking back, I don't take that from any of them. Not even the oldest. . . . They can express their opinions, they can raise their voices a little, but not this answering back. They must give respect.

"The most important thing I try to teach them is to love one another, and try to help one another. . . . It's not like you get a job and you're just helping yourself, make money, make money. You don't want that. You have to make money, because you have to live—but if you can do it and help somebody at the same time, then you're doing good. Sometimes they see it, and sometimes they don't. But you've got to keep trying."

Mrs. C's own words express more eloquently than we can the set of values that consistently guide her rearing of Cathy. Hearing her speak, we find it hard to come to any categorical conclusion about the value of Cathy's environment, despite the obvious lack of material apparatus and maternal stimulation that our research study finds to be most important to a child's intellectual advancement. As we reflect on our observations on Cathy and her mother's remarks, it seems to us that the training in social responsibility that her mother provides—training in understanding the points of view and needs of others, training to collaborate, to cooperate and to share with others—may be more fundamental to the child's development in the long run, although given the particular focus of our research it may not seem so. Our own emphasis on seeing the intellectual rather than the social or moral value of the child's experiences, and indeed our very definition of what is or is not an intellectually valuable experience are called into question. An observation that we made on *Brenda* whose *intellectual* development seemed so well provided for vividly makes our point.

At the time Brenda is about two-and-a-half years old. We find her mother reading her the well-known story of Babar the elephant, recounting Babar's honeymoon trip in a balloon with his bride, Celeste, the wrecking of the balloon on a lonely island, and the attack made by the inhabitants of the island who are finally put to flight by Babar.° Mrs. B is a skillful reader. She makes the story come alive with dramatic emphasis (the inhabitants are *"fierce and savage cannibals"*), with apt elaboration ("See, Brenda: they want to eat up Celeste's soft pink meat"), with histrionic gestures ("Celeste sighs sadly, she thinks soon she will be eaten"— Mother moans; "They both hurl themselves at the cannibals. Some are wounded, others take flight; all are terrified"—Mother rolls her eyes). Brenda is engrossed. She repeats her mother's words from time to time ("Eat up her meat"); she asks questions ("The men kill her? Babar come back?"); her eyes and face are alive with emotion. One can almost see the images impressing themselves one by one on her senses. Her mind and imagination seem totally engaged. It is for her an intellectual experience *par excellence.*

°Jean DeBrunhoff, *Travels of Babar* (New York: Random House, 1934). According to a personal communication from Laurent DeBrunhoff, this section of the cannibals is being excised from future editions.

But now we ask: What is the social message of the story? What, actually, is Brenda learning? What will she remember? The savages are *black*. They come to attack Celeste with their sharp *spears*. They desire to eat her *soft pink* flesh. Babar, the hero, puts them to terrified flight with a few sure blows. What is Brenda learning?

It took Mrs. B many minutes before it seemed to dawn on her to just what end she might be putting her considerable skills. As the savages escaped in gibbering flight, Brenda's mother suddenly looked up and saw that the observer faithfully recording this episode was black, thick-lipped, broad-nosed, bushy-haired, as were the cannibals in the illustrations. Mrs. B blushed, fumbled with her book, looked up again, hesitated. Brenda's eyes followed her mother's gaze. "Come on, Mommy. Read the story," she demanded.

7

Vicky:
An Extreme Environment

So far we have described six fairly benign environments in which we observed young children growing up. These environments differed certainly on intellectual, social, and emotional dimensions and differences among them were apparently correlated with the children's development in these areas. Some offered a rich base for intellectual development (for example Brenda's home), others a secure context for social and emotional development (for example Cathy's home), others seemed to provide both (for example Sonja's and Matthew's homes), and others relatively little of either (for example Diana's home). What we have not yet included are examples of environments that seem *absolutely*, not merely relatively, deleterious to the child's development—examples of environments that, by almost any reasonable standard (not necessarily the particular ones used in this study), seem likely to retard or distort a child's intellectual, social, and emotional growth.

In our final case studies we turn to two such examples. In the first we shall describe an environment that seems mostly to be of the mother's making. No doubt this mother has serious psychological problems herself, that may be the main cause of her frequently harsh, occasionally terrifying treatment of her children. We do not know precisely what these problems are, because we did not delve into her personal history and know only what she or her husband chose to tell us. What we do know about is how she actually behaved toward her children—specifically her one-year-old daughter, Vicky—and how the human environment she created seemed to affect Vicky's development over the course of the two years that we visited the home. As always, the focus of our case studies is less on the reasons why certain environments come about than in their consequences for the children who live in them.

The second of our last pair of case studies is also an example of an extreme environment—extreme in the sense of being undeniably harmful to Terry, our child-subject. But this case differs from Vicky's in that here the child himself exhibits from a very young age definite psychological and intellectual malfunctioning that would make it difficult for any ordinary mother to help create an appropriate human or physical environment for him. But Terry's mother, like Vicky's, has psychological problems of her own; and these so aggravate the problem that child and mother seem caught in a trap in which both present extreme, negative human environments for each other that neither can successfully adapt to or change. We shall present Vicky's story in this chapter and Terry's in the next.

SOCIOECONOMIC AND CULTURAL BACKGROUND

Vicky's father works as a housepainter and his income from seasonal employment is less than $3,000 for a family of two adults and four children. Vicky's mother completed eleventh grade in the Boston school system, whereas her father went only as far as seventh grade in the South. The family lives in an apartment in a large public-housing project in Boston. Their apartment consists of three bedrooms, living room, kitchen, and bath. Although shabby and gloomy by middle-class standards, it is maintained in fair condition, and there are no particular signs of structural or surface deterioration. The housing project in which the apartment is located is crowded and gives a dilapidated impression, with paint peeling off the walls, trash blowing about the yard areas, and very little safe space or equipment for children to play with. The vast majority of the residents of the project are white, poor, and of limited education like Vicky's parents.

Mr. and Mrs. V have four children who were six (Tracy), five (Joey), three (Randy), and one (Vicky) when we started visiting in their home. When we began our observations on Vicky, the oldest girl, Tracy, was attending kindergarten while the other three children were at home with their mother. Two years later when we concluded our observations, all three older children were in school or pre-school and only Vicky spent all day at home with her mother.

Vicky's family was brought to our attention through the aegis of a well-baby clinic (as were several other families in the study). A check with her older sister's teacher found that Tracy was "below average" in school performance and showed a "clear lack of readiness for school," although "she adjusted well to special help." Early impressions of observers in the home were consistent with the teacher's ratings of Vicky's older sister who, in fact, seemed better developed intellectually than her brothers. In particular, Vicky's younger brother's speech was clearly immature and often unintelligible to a stranger.

VICKY'S INTELLECTUAL DEVELOPMENT

Vicky's performance on the Bayley test at age twelve months was about average (Mental Development Index $= 97$). She maintained this standing until age two (Mental Development Index $= 97$) but by age three her performance, now assessed by the Stanford Binet, was considerably poorer relative to standardized norms (IQ $= 76$). Her performance on the less well-standardized tests of receptive language and spatial abilities placed her in the last quartile relative to our sample from age one and consistently thereafter.

VICKY'S MOTHER

The most striking thing about Vicky's home to an observer was its emotionally-charged atmosphere. The immediate reason for this seemed to be the personality of Vicky's mother. Highly emotional, frequently hostile, given to sudden changes in mood, Mrs. V dominated the lives of Vicky and her brothers and sister, constantly creating tension, fear, anger, and diffuse excitement. Mrs. V's children seemed to have very few moments of privacy, freedom, or security. Their play was often interrupted by their mother's arbitrary restrictions; their persons threatened by her promises to "kill," "cremate," "croak" them, or to "flatten a nose," "break an arm," "crush a skull"; their bodies bruised by her actual use of such physical punishment as slaps, chops around the ear, pinches, and beltings.

Mrs. V believed her children to be "born bad" and sought to knock the evil out of them; but what they seemed to respond to was not so much her violent methods as her image of them. She expected them to be and this is how they often acted—disobedient, destructive, disrespectful, and "dumb." Intimidated by her threats and punishments, Mrs. V's children did not usually challenge her directly. More often they deflected their resentment to each other in squabbling, inflicting petty cruelties, teasing, telling tales, and playing each other off to gain a temporary advantage. This pattern of behavior repeated itself from child to child, though with significant variations. The importance of Vicky's story is that we began observing her when she was very young and thus were able to see the very traits her mother considered inborn emerge before our very eyes under her tutelage. The fascinating details of this tutoring and the pupil's response to it are easily discernible in our moment-to-moment observations on Vicky and may be organized in terms of a few major themes. Let us consider these in turn.

INTELLECTUAL STIMULATION

Intellectual stimulation is noteworthy in Vicky's home more for its absence than for its presence. There are only a few instances in our observations of experiences that might be judged intellectually valuable for Vicky. The most clear-cut of these occur with Vicky's father. On one occasion he showed her how to blow up a doughnut-shaped balloon and encouraged her to experiment putting it on and off her head. On another occasion he encouraged her to open and close a difficult-to-fit box flap, a task that called for a fair degree of fine-motor coordination and understanding of spatial relationships in a two-year-old. Most of the remaining few instances occur with Vicky's mother, but here an important feature needs to be noted: Almost all of Vicky's intellectual experiences with her mother seem to occur in a semihostile context in which her mother seems to be disparaging the task in question or annoyed at Vicky for other reasons. Here are some examples of what we mean.

Vicky: Excerpt 1

At the time of this observation Vicky was twenty-four months old. Mother is changing her in the bathroom after Vicky has had an "accident" in her panties.

> Mother: "Did you ka-ka again?" Mother undresses Vicky asking in an irritated way, "Why didn't you tell me pottie, you can say pottie."
> Vicky obligingly says "pottie." Mother: "Yeah, now when it doesn't do any good. I'm getting tired of you. Turn around." Mother washes her. Vicky: "Ka-ka." Mother: "Yeah, ka-ka—you're bad. You're supposed to say pottie, bad girl. Turn around." Mother washes Vicky. Vicky: "Ka-ka." Mother: "Ka-ka's right!" Vicky: "Ick." Mother: "Right." Vicky spits. Mother: "I'll slap you!"
> Vicky chokes. Mother: "What do you have in your mouth?" Vicky shows her a piece of doughnut. Mother: "Here, put your tights on, you don't need your pants." Mother: "Come on, bad baby." Vicky: "These." Mother: "Yeah. Come over here." (On to the toilet.) Vicky climbs up on the toilet seat. She struggles. Mother: "You know how to get up there. You're bad. Bad baby. Bad." Vicky: "Baby." Mother: **"You're** the bad baby. Give me one (foot). I don't want two, give me one." Vicky holds up an indeterminate number of fingers and asks, "Two?"

Vicky holds out one foot. Mother puts tights on one leg. Mother: "Give me two now." Vicky holds up her other foot. Mother: "Yeah, that's two." Mother pulls up Vicky's tights and sets her down. Mother: "Bad." Vicky: "Bad baby." Mother: "Yeah, bad baby." Mother tells Vicky she doesn't need her pants on because she has on tights. Mother: "Go play." Vicky runs down the hallway toward her father.

Vicky: Excerpt 2

This observation was made nine months later when Vicky was thirty-three months old. Vicky and her mother have been play-fighting and Vicky is sitting on her mother's lap, as her two brothers gawk at the rare privilege of reciprocal aggression and affection conferred on Vicky.

Mother says to Vicky, "What's your name?" Vicky (emboldened perhaps by her previous liberties with her mother): "Ka-Ka, Ma-Ma." Mother (smiling): "What's your other name? What's your other name, Vic-Vic?" Vicky: "Ka-Ka." Mother taps her arm, scolding. Vicky giggles and repeats, "Ka-Ka." Mother: "You're acting up!"

Mother: "What's your name Vic-Vic? What's your other name?" Vicky: "Ka-Ka! Ka-Ka!" Vicky drinks from her bottle. Mother: "What's your name?" Vicky: "Ka-Ka." Mother taps Vicky on the mouth, half-threateningly. Vicky: "Vic-Vic." Mother: "Victoria!"

Vicky: "Vic-Vic." Mother: "Victoria Mandeville." Vicky (defiantly): "Ka-Ka." Mother hits Vicky on the arm. Vicky: "Mandeville." Mother (threateningly): "Now, what's your name?" Vicky (defiantly): "Ka-Ka." Mother hits Vicky harder and she whimpers. Mother: "Now what's your name?" Vicky (in tears): "Ka-Ka." Mother hits Vicky again.

Mother, raising her voice loudly and glaring at Vicky: "Now, put your head up and talk!" Mother threatens to swipe Vicky's brother, Randy, if he doesn't shut up. Mother turns back to Vicky: "What's your name?" Vicky: "Vic-Vic." Mother (sternly): "What's your name? Say Mandeville." Vicky: "Vic-Vic." Mother: "Mandeville." Vicky (softly): "Mandeville."

Mother: "Say it again." Vicky: "Bum-Bum." Mother: "I'm going to stop playing with you if you don't act very well!" Vicky pouts defiantly. Mother: "What's your name?" Vicky: "Mandeville." Mother: "Victoria Mary Mandeville." Vicky repeats sulkily: "Victoria Mary Mandeville."

Mother: "What's Sparky's (one of their dogs) name?" Vicky: "Sparky." Mother: "Mandeville." Vicky mumbles, perhaps repeating the name. Vicky lies back sucking on her bottle.

Commentary. In both excerpts Vicky's mother seems intent on compelling Vicky to perform correctly perhaps to impress the observer but more likely to satisfy her own need to exert power. In the first excerpt Vicky's little accomplishments (saying "pottie," struggling to climb up on the toilet, "counting") evoke mostly comments of "bad girl." In the second observation the right answer is literally forced from the defiant Vicky on pain of punishment, her mother prolonging the badgering until the child is cowed into submission. Whatever Vicky may have learned from this

interchange, it certainly did not seem to be how to say her name. The real
lesson for Vicky seemed to be a social one. She learned something about
the limits of her own freedom set by the needs of her volatile, insecure,
and hostile mother and she learned something about how to manipulate
these needs for her own survival. Vicky learned this lesson well, eventually
turning it to advantage, as we shall see in a later episode.

AGGRESSION

The theme of aggression overrides all others in our observations of Vicky.
Vicky was exposed to it in many forms both direct and indirect. In its
most direct guise, Vicky observed her mother constantly scolding her
brothers, using abusive language, making outrageous threats, and frequently physically punishing them. She herself was also frequently
scolded, threatened, insulted, and spanked by her mother and victimized
by her brothers who teased her, took away her toys, mocked, and hit her.
In retaliation she sneaked away her brothers' possessions, told tales, and,
as she grew older and stronger, learned to hit them back, pick fights, and
even to use them as scapegoats to escape punishment for her own mis-
demeanors. We begin our discussion of this theme with three excerpts
illustrating the belligerent and arbitrary style typically adopted by Vicky's
mother.

Vicky: Excerpt 3

Vicky is just thirteen months old at the time of this visit. Her mother is
more restrained than usual, since this is our first observation in her home
and presumably she is seeking to make a favorable impression.

> Vicky shakes the leg of a desk. Mother: "No! No! That is not a toy." Vicky
> looks at her mother and continues shaking the desk leg. Mother observes
> her and says, "Come here." Vicky ignores this and continues shaking the
> leg. Mother repeats, "Come here." Vicky ignores her and continues.
>   Mother looks at the TV. Mother: "Vicky, no!" Her brother, Joey, tries to
> block Vicky. Mother: "No, Vicky. Bad baby!"

Vicky: Excerpt 4

Vicky is now two months older. Her mother has warned her not to go
into the bedroom where a neighbor's baby is sleeping, but curiosity over-
comes the child.

> Vicky goes down the hall toward the bedroom. Mother sees her and shrieks
> from the living room, "You little pig! I'll spank you, you ———! Get in here!"
> Vicky continues on her way to the bedroom. Mother races to the bedroom

and removes Vicky bodily. Mother: "Bad baby!" Vicky returns down the hall with her mother close behind. She shows no emotional reaction to her mother's behavior. Later, after an interruption, we find Vicky's mother sitting on the couch, Vicky standing nearby fiddling with an empty toilet-paper roll.

Vicky walks down the hall to the bedroom again. Mother follows without Vicky seeing her, but stops at the kitchen.

Vicky goes into the bedroom and pulls the baby's blanket. Her brother Randy has also sneaked in and joins Vicky in pulling the blanket. Mother comes in, slaps Randy and shouts to both, "Get out of here now!" Vicky goes out of the bedroom, then comes in again. Mother: "Get out!" and pushes her out. Vicky goes into the adjoining bathroom.

Mother: "Get out of that bath! I'll beat **your** ass too! Out! Out!" and slaps Vicky hard on the bottom. Vicky moves quietly to the hall. Mother: "Get in there (the living room) or I'll get the strap!" Vicky moves off.

Vicky: Excerpt 5

Vicky, age nineteen months, is being toilet trained. This is how her mother sets about it.

Mother calls Vicky over. Mother: "Did you go pee-pee?" Vicky pulls her pants down. Mother: "Did you go pee-pee?" Vicky shakes her head. Mother: "Get up on the couch so I can change you."

Mother changes Vicky's diaper on the couch. Mother (very irritated): "You want me to slap you? Peeing in your pants. . . ." Mother powders Vicky and continues scolding. Vicky clasps her doll to her chest.

Vicky squeezes the doll and it makes a crying noise. Mother imitates the noise, puts Vicky on the floor and pulls up her pants. Mother: "Bad baby!" as she gets up to put the dirty diaper away.

"BAD BABY"

The use of such terms as "bad baby," "monster," and so on need not, of course, be interpreted literally. Several mothers in our study used just these words to convey not condemnation but affection or admiration. Still others used them simply to correct a particular bit of behavior they disapproved of and the terms seemed to have no more consequence than if they had merely said "no." In Vicky's case, however, these terms were so constantly, vehemently, and gratuitously employed that they seemed to be a real indictment of her character. At least this is how Vicky seemed to interpret their use. Thus, in several observations we find Vicky struggling with the notion of herself as "bad." She sometimes accepts, sometimes rejects this verdict, and sometimes she resolves the conflict rather shrewdly by projecting the term onto others, notably her mother and her mother's apparent favorite in the household, the dog. Consider the following episodes.

Vicky: Excerpt 6

Vicky is now age twenty-six months. She is still undergoing the trials and tribulations of toilet training and has had yet another unfortunate "accident."

> Some feces drop out of Vicky's pants. Mother: "Come on, let's go to the bathroom." Vicky points to the dropping on the floor and babbles. Mother: "Come on, let's go to the bathroom right now."
> Mother: "Come on. Go ahead." Vicky follows slowly, walking stifly as another dropping falls to the floor. Vicky comments, "Ka-Ka." Mother: "Yes." Vicky: "Mommy bad." Mother: "No, not Mommy, **you** are bad. You **are** bad, you know." Mother looks on as more feces fall from Vicky's pants and says, "Don't move, you are dropping them all over." (Mother changes Vicky and wipes up the mess.)
> Vicky: "Bad, bad puppy." Mother: "No, bad, bad **Vicky.** Vicky is bad." Vicky (protesting): "Puppy, puppy!" Mother: **"Vicky,** not puppy." Vicky follows Mother out of the kitchen and pulls Mother's belt at her back, babbling. Mother tickles Vicky's bottom. Vicky squats down and feels the leg of a chair where the puppy had earlier chewed it and says, "Puppy."
> Mother: "Puppy did not do it, Vicky did it." (Referring, apparently, to Vicky's bowel movement.) Vicky: "No, puppy," pointing to the chair. Vicky gets up from the floor and says, "Ka-ka." Mother: "Are you all cleaned up?" Vicky: "Yeah." Mother: "Yeah?" Vicky sits on the floor and looks at the bottom of her shoes on which some feces are stuck. Vicky shows her shoes to a visitor. (Female friend of her mother's.) Visitor: "You have something on your shoes?" Vicky: **"Mama** did it." Visitor: "Mama did it? Wow!"

Vicky: Excerpt 7

Five months later when she is thirty-one months old Vicky is still struggling to reject the idea of herself as "bad."

> Vicky: "Babies." (Referring, apparently, to the mess created by a newly acquired puppy that she and her mother are petting.) Mother: "No, you kids make more mess than all the dogs in the kitchen." (The family now has three dogs.) Mother fixes Vicky's sock. Mother: "You're a bad girl." Vicky (emphatically): "Not bad girl, not bad girl!" Mother: "Oh, not bad?"
> Vicky: "Bad **boy.**" (Pointing to the puppy.) Mother: "Why is he bad? Is Vicky bad?" Vicky: **"Mommy's** bad."

Vicky: Excerpt 8

Finally, two months later, we have this observation.

> Mother: "What do you want Santa to bring you (for Christmas)?" Vicky: "A dog." Mother: "You already have one." Mother repeats, "What do you want Santa to bring you?" Vicky: "Nothing." Mother: "Really?" Vicky: "You are bad." Mother: "No, **you** are bad. . ." Three-and-a-half minutes elapse.
> Mother (returning to the topic after an interruption): "I thought you wanted

a doll-carriage?" Vicky: "No, I'm bad." Mother: "Not you, **they** (Vicky's brothers) are the bad ones." Vicky: "Me, bad one." Mother laughs.

Commentary. It is easy to read too much into a child's sayings. Children of this age sometimes play games with words and what they say may not be as ominous as it sounds. However, Vicky's frequent application of the term "bad" to herself, to her mother, and to the mother's favorite pet in many different contexts compels us to ask what sort of image of herself she is constructing and also what sort of picture of her mother she is gradually forming. Another point is worth noting. Vicky is now just at the age when we might expect her to show jealousy of her mother and possessiveness of her father, two developments that may be influencing her judgment of her mother as "bad" along with other more realistic considerations. But Vicky's budding identification with her father and her appealing to him for protection are also a source of irritation for her mother, as the next two excerpts illustrate.

Vicky: Excerpt 9
Vicky is now about nineteen months.

> Vicky climbs up on a rocker. Mother (angry): "Not that way!" and slaps Vicky. Father comes in. Vicky whines to Father, apparently complaining about Mother. Mother explains to Father that Vicky might have hurt herself by climbing on the rocker that way.
> Vicky continues to whimper. Mother to Vicky: "I didn't hit you that hard! Go ahead, tell your father!" (Delivered like a taunt.) Vicky wanders off.

Vicky: Excerpt 10
And again when Vicky is twenty-five months.

> Father: "You are Daddy's girl?" Vicky: "Yeah." Vicky calls to her mother: "Baba." Mother: "No you can't take your baba (bottle) out."
> Vicky pouts. Mother: "You love your Daddy, so stop picking on me!" Father makes funny faces at Vicky and she laughs. Three minutes later, after an interruption:
> Mother to Vicky: "Let me sit down." (Vicky is sprawled across an armchair.) Vicky: "No." Mother (smiling): "I could sit on Daddy!"
> Mother holds Father's hand. Vicky pulls Mother's hand away and grabs Father's. Mother and Father comment, "Look at that!" Mother touches Father's hand, Vicky pushes it away again. They laugh.

Commentary. We are tempted to interpret Vicky's behavior in the last excerpt as illustrating a normal developmental stage in the life of a two-year-old girl but for an important occurrence that we have not mentioned so far; a few months before this observation Mrs. V had left her husband to live with someone else and all the children understood (in some sense) why she had left. In fact, (according to the father's report) they were given the choice by their mother in a stormy last scene to go with her or stay with their father, and they all opted to stay. During the three months that Mrs. V was away from her family, Mr. V had had full responsibility for looking after the children and, as far as we could tell from the two observations that we made while he was in charge, treated Vicky and her siblings with considerably more affection, gentleness, and good humor than had his wife. Thus Vicky's jealousy and possessiveness are probably not a simple matter of a daughter suddenly discovering the pleasures of being with father. Her resentment against her mother is based not merely on the comparison she must be making between her parents but also on her mother's display of favoritism toward her pet dogs. Vicky's growing resentment of these animals is unmasked several times in our observations, as in the following excerpt.

Vicky: Excerpt 11

Vicky, now thirty-two months old, is with her mother petting the dogs.

> Vicky says something (unclear). Mother: "Who is going to bite me?" Vicky: "Fannie." (One of the dogs.) Mother: "No, the dogs love me, they won't bite me." Vicky: "Not your dog." Mother: **"My** Sparky, **my** Fannie." (Referring to the dogs.) Vicky squeezes one of the dogs. Mother: "No, it will bite you."
> Vicky pinches the dog. Mother: "Stop!" Vicky now pinches her Mother. Mother: "No!" Vicky stops.

AFFECTION

It will be no surprise for the reader to learn that Vicky's family showed relatively little overt affection toward her. Her father and older sister seemed to enjoy her the most and occasionally stroked, cuddled, and romped with her in a genuinely affectionate and loving fashion. Her experiences with her mother were more complicated. First, in several instances during our visits her mother made an affectionate overture to Vicky that the child spurned—a rather unusual occurrence in our observations of children this young. One reason for this may be that her mother tended to approach Vicky with a *demand* that she show her affection inevitably evoking obstinacy. If she had simply expressed affection toward Vicky, the child might have responded differently. But Vicky's rebuffs to her mother probably reflected a growing resentment of her, as well as a glimmering understanding of ways to retaliate against her for wrongs received. Consider the following observations.

Vicky: Excerpt 12

Mother, Vicky, age fifteen months, and the other three children are in the living room. The TV is on and the other children are playing a card game.

> Mother tells Vicky to dance. Vicky starts to shake more or less in time to the music coming from the television. Mother smiles and calls to Vicky to go to her. Mother: "Give me a kiss." Vicky walks away. Mothers calls, "Vicky." Vicky ignores her as she watches the TV. Mother comes over and hugs Vicky.

Vicky: Excerpt 13

Nine months later, when Vicky is two, a more ambiguous interchange occurs.

> Mother asks Vicky for a kiss, saying, "I didn't get one this morning." Vicky refuses: "No," and laughs. Vicky stands up. Mother: "Sit down. Now, give me a kiss." Vicky turns her head away, perhaps seriously, perhaps as a game.

Commentary.   These two observations may seem rather unremarkable. So what if Vicky does not want her mother to embrace her? Most children rebuff their parents' kisses and cuddles some of the time and this is hardly significant if, on other occasions, they seek out, receive, and return affection with evident pleasure. The problem in Vicky's case is that we encountered extremely few instances in which affection, pure and simple, was exchanged with her mother. Almost all the instances of affection that we came across, when not ignored by Vicky, were embedded in a context of play-fighting/play-teasing in which the mood of the interchange fluctuated uncertainly between affection and hostility, so much so that the observers were often hard put to decide which was actually being conveyed. In addition there was always an element of compulsion to these interactions between Mrs. V and Vicky. The subtext of most of them implied a power-play on the part of the mother and a struggle to learn the rules and manipulate the system on the part of the daughter. Two most vivid examples of the complex dynamics that characterized Vicky's so-called playful interchanges with her mother are given in the following excerpts, quoted at length.

Vicky: Excerpt 14

Vicky is twenty-five months old.

> Mother: "Are you my lover? Then give me a kiss. If you don't you won't get no supper." Vicky goes over to Mother and her mother kisses her. Vicky slaps Mother's bottom.
> Vicky tries to pinch Mother on the bottom and Mother laughs. Vicky pinches Mother's back. Mother: "Don't pull my hair." Vicky makes a loud

noise and folds her arms in a gesture of toughness. Mother: "You are not big enough to fight with me."

A visiting friend of her mother's asks Vicky to put away an empty milk can. Vicky takes it to the nearby garbage pail. Vicky resumes her game with her mother and slaps her on the arm. Visitor: "That's a big one!" Mother pretends to cry. Vicky hugs Mother, apparently as part of the ritual.

Mother: "Oh, you hurt my hand." Vicky pulls out Mother's hand and kisses the thumb. Vicky climbs up and sits next to Mother.

Vicky picks up a belt from the table and pats Mother's arm with it. Mother pretends to cry and Vicky hugs Mother's head. Vicky again folds her arms in an "I am tough" gesture. Mother laughs. She now pinches Mother's nose. Mother (laughing): "No."

Visitor: "You can go 'peep-peep'," and demonstrates, pressing Vicky's nose and making a squeaking sound. Vicky imitates, doing the same to Mother's nose. Mother laughs.

Commentary. This appears to be a very pleasant, basically affectionate interchange in which Mrs. V and Vicky are evidently enjoying the spanks, pinches, and mock-threats much as another couple might enjoy cuddles, kisses, and terms of endearment. But, as we shall see, the balance between affection and hostility in Vicky's many play-fights with her mother is often easily upset. Consider the next excerpt taken from an observation made when Vicky was thirty-two months old.

Vicky: Excerpt 15

Vicky is drinking a bottle of juice. She takes the nipple out of her mouth and shakes her head. Mother tickles her and shakes her body playfully. Vicky (seriously): "Don't touch me." Vicky swings her legs around Mother who says, "Don't hurt Sparky." (The dog.) Vicky moves her leg out of the dog's way and Mother touches Vicky affectionately.

Vicky to Mother (scowling): "Don't touch me." Mother (glaring back): "Then I won't feed you, won't give you no supper." Vicky: **"I won't feed you."** Mother: "I am the one who does the cooking here." Vicky (protesting): "I cook. I cook the spaghetti sauce." Mother: "Yes, you did."

Vicky looks on as Mother talks to the dogs. She deliberately touches one of the dogs with her foot. Mother: "Don't kick it." Vicky: "I won't feed you." Mother: "See if I care." Vicky: "I'll go to the hospital." Mother: (half tauntingly) "Aren't you tired of going there?" (Vicky has recently had several teeth extracted at the clinic.)

Vicky puts her bottle on the coffee table and babbles something. Mother: "What, honey?" Vicky pinches her mother's foot. Mother: "Stop it! Go watch Randy." (Vicky's brother.) Vicky pinches her mother again. Mother slaps her hand and Vicky whimpers.

Vicky pulls her pants down. Mother: "Pull it up!" Mother chases Vicky around the coffee table, saying, "Come over here!" Vicky whines, "You beat me." Mother: "No, I am not going to." Vicky: "I won't feed you." Mother: "I do the cooking here. . ."

Commentary.   This is clearly a much more complex scene to analyze than the previous superficially similar example of play-teasing. The reasons are several. First is the abrupt changes in mood on the part of Mrs. V. Her initial playful approach to Vicky quickly becomes threatening and punitive when the child rejects her overture ("I won't feed you."), softens as she apparently tries to humor Vicky, then hardens again as Vicky acts out her resentment by kicking her. A second reason is the ambiguity of intention. It is very difficult to tell from Mrs. V's behavior both verbal and nonverbal exactly what message she means to convey to Vicky. For example, when she asks Vicky whether she isn't tired of going to the hospital we give Mrs. V the benefit of the doubt and assume she is trying to humor Vicky. But the words may also be meant to hurt (i.e., "Go to the hospital and see how you like it"!) in the same way as the mother's previous retort ("See if I care"!) is apparently intended to wound. The third factor complicating the interpretation of this scene is the use of power. Mother threatens Vicky with loss of food if she does not let her fondle her (this is not an idle threat since Mrs. V does deprive her children of food as punishment), and Vicky retaliates with similar threats, powerless though she is to implement them. Her mother seems intent on exerting control through the use of power, whereas Vicky seems to be struggling to understand her mother's idiosyncrasies and to manipulate the shifting system of rules and expectancies for her own survival. Nowhere are these themes more dramatically evident than in our final observation made when Vicky was thirty-three months old.

Vicky: Excerpt 16

The observation started with Vicky and her mother play-fighting in the living room. Her brothers, Joey and Randy, are in bad grace with their mother and Randy, in particular, has been expressly forbidden to open his mouth or come near her. The two boys crouch in the corners of the living room, gawking at the spectacle of their baby sister entertaining their mother by fighting with her, a privilege they can hardly hope to obtain for themselves. Occasionally Randy strays too close to the scene and Mrs. V peremptorily slaps him away. We pick up the action at a point when the original positive mood has turned sour and Vicky has had a lesson in the limits to which she can go in opposing her mother even in play. (see excerpt 2.)

> Vicky sucks her bottle sulkily. She looks at TV and at Mother threatening her brother Randy. Mother to Randy: "Shut up! Or it's bed for you right now."
> Vicky continues drinking and listening to Mother threaten Randy.
> Vicky drinks from her bottle sleepily, then sits up as Mother says to Randy, "That's it! It's the tape for you!" Mother rushes to a table in the hall to get

some sticky brown paper tape. Mother to Randy: "I'm tired of you. I've been threatening to tape your mouth up for three weeks." Vicky scurries over and holds Randy's head to help her mother do the taping. Mother wets then stretches about three inches of tape over Randy's mouth.

Randy, whimpering, pulls off the tape from his mouth. Mother: "Want me to get some regular tape? (Scotch tape rather than the paper tape she's been using.) That'll hurt plenty more!" Randy mumbles a plea (apparently promising to shut up). Vicky struggles to smooth out the used strip of tape.

Mother sticks pieces of Scotch tape on the coffee table. Vicky looks on. Vicky: "Why you do that?" Mother: "The next time he (Randy) opens his mouth, I'm going to use this on him." Vicky: "Randy," pointing to him (apparently telling Mother that Randy is whispering). Randy sits several feet away looking at TV and mumbling to himself. Mother: "He's pushing his luck!" Mother and Vicky look at Randy to see if he's really talking. Vicky: "Tape," and tries to pull off a piece of tape from the table (as if preparing to go and tape Randy's mouth). Mother: "No."

Vicky: "Tape." Mother: "I've got the tape in my hand, ready for him." Vicky: "Tape." Mother: "That's for Randy's mouth, that's his gag." Vicky: "I want to hold it." Mother: "No! I'll give you another piece to hold." Mother gives her a piece of tape. Mother: "That's it, no more tape."

Vicky: "I hold it." Vicky tries to smooth out the tape, as it sticks to her fingers. Vicky: "Tape." She continues trying to smooth out the tape. Vicky to Mother: "Hard." (Regarding the tape.) Mother doesn't answer. Vicky struggles to smooth out the tape. Vicky goes to Randy and tries to tape his mouth. He laughs. Mother: "Get away! I'll tape his mouth. He won't think it's so funny then!"

Vicky continues trying to tape Randy's mouth. Mother suddenly swoops over to Randy, sits on him, and pins him down. She tapes his mouth with a piece of Scotch tape. (Randy is spread eagled on the floor with Mother sitting on top and Vicky helping, holding down his arm.) Randy struggles, whimpering. Vicky gleefully brings Mother another piece of tape to put on Randy's mouth. Mother: "I don't need it. This will hurt enough coming off. Won't it?" (Derisively to Randy.) Vicky offers more tape to Mother.

Mother to Vicky: "You can leave him alone." Mother to Randy: "You gonna stop talking? Eh? Eh?" Randy nods, whimpering, as he's pinned down on the floor. Mother rips off the tape. Mother: "It hurts coming off, don't it!" Randy whimpers. Vicky: "I'll put it on (again)!" Mother: "No, no." Vicky tries to put some tape on her other brother, Joey. Vicky continues. Joey allows her to (indulging her playfully). Mother admonishes Vicky: "Don't stick it!"

Joey: "It don't hurt me." Mother laughs: "She got the stickiness out! You gotta press it down." Mother (glaring) to Randy: "You want more tape?" (Randy may have mumbled something to bring on this threat but, if so, the observer did not hear him.) Randy: "No," plaintively. Vicky continues trying to tape Joey's mouth. Vicky: "Tape." (Asking for more tape.) Mother: "There's more right there." (On the table.)

Vicky now puts some tape on Mother's neck. Mother: "You put it on my hair and I'll slap you!" Vicky tapes Mother's face. Mother: "You silly." (Laughing. Mother is lying on the couch allowing Vicky to do this.) Mother: "You silly. You're holding the sticky part." (I.e., not putting the sticky part on Mother.) Vicky continues applying tape to Mother's arm and face.

Vicky to Mother: "I put it on there! (Mother's blouse.) Ma! Ma!" (Mother has her head down and doesn't respond to Vicky.) Vicky pulls Mother's head up to make her attend. Mother looks at the tape on her blouse and giggles. Vicky hits Mother lightly on the arm. Mother: "You hit me." Vicky taps Mother on the nose. Mother (smiling): "Hey, my nose." Mother to dog: "Get her, Sparky. She's bothering me." Vicky continues hitting Mother playfully. Mother to dog: "Get her. Get her off."

Mother to Vicky: "Sparky wants to kiss you." Vicky cuddles the dog. Vicky tries to smooth out a piece of Scotch tape.

Vicky to Mother: "I'll tape your mouth!" She tapes Mother's mouth. Mother tapes Vicky's mouth playfully. Vicky: "I'll tape yours." (Vicky is really sticking down the tape and it may be hurting her mother.)Vicky tapes Mother's mouth. Mother (sounding irritated): "Now go play with your brother for a while." Vicky continues taping her Mother's mouth. (Observation ends.)

Commentary. To the observer who witnessed this scene the most remarkable thing so far as Vicky was concerned was her extraordinary skill in handling her mother. For the most part (except when her obstinacy got the better of her as in excerpt 15), Vicky displayed exquisite sensitivity to her mother's moods, delicately treading the thin line between Mrs. V's interest and her anger.

Most of the observation (only part of which is reported here) consisted of play-fighting between Vicky and her mother. This seemed to be undertaken by Mrs. V almost as a spectacle to impress Vicky's brothers with the sense of their own impotency and disfavor. Each time one of the brothers tried to join in or come closer to the action he was summarily ordered away with a threat by his mother to "kill," "cremate," "bash his head in," "crack his knuckles" and so on, threats delivered with contempt if not with real intent to terrify. Throughout the message rang clear that, temporarily at least, Vicky had come into her mother's good grace whereas the boys remained in limbo.

The immediate context for Vicky's ascendance seemed to be that the older boy, Joey, had feigned sickness that morning to avoid going to school. His mother had telephoned his teacher and found out that a classmate had been bullying him and that Joey, instead of standing up to the boy, had acted like a "sissy." Joey, therefore, had to be punished for his cowardice and malingering and Randy for some other undisclosed misbehavior by being forbidden to play or talk. They were also to be taught how sweet was the privilege of being in their mother's favor—a privilege they would see conferred on their baby sister but that they could not hope to attain. This lesson was impressed on the boys when at one point Joey tried to join in the play-fight only to be slapped away by Mrs. V with the taunt: "Get away! You're jealous of her. You want to be the baby and sit in my lap. You sissy, you!"

The theme of favoritism emerged again after the observation was over and Mrs. V boasted, in front of the boys, that Vicky was much

brighter than her brothers who were "real dum-dums." Mrs. V then pro-
ceded to prove this by asking Vicky to say the names of various objects
in the house—lamp, drier, washer, and so on—and to show where objects
like her mother's cigarettes, money, and keys were kept. Urged on by her
mother's praise and oblivious of her brothers' silent envy. Vicky performed
admirably. Finally, Mrs. V invited the observer to her bedroom where she
placed on the bed an ornate jewel box, complete with tiny drawers and
glittering mesh gates. With her brothers banished to the far corner
of the room, their eyes bulging with desire to touch the forbidden trinkets,
Vicky was then asked to name the ornaments that her mother took out
one by one from the inside of the jewel box. Holding up now a necklace,
now a ring, now a shimmering bracelet, Vicky pronounced their names
and adorned her chubby body with the jewelry. "Fabulous! You look like
a princess," acclaimed her mother, as Vicky, lapping up her admiration,
preened and strutted before her brothers.

It would be dishonest of us not to acknowledge that this was one of
the most unpleasant observations we made during the three years we took
to complete our research study. It was hard not to see Mrs. V's behavior
toward her sons as cruel, her favoritism of Vicky as self-serving. It was
a deeply upsetting experience for the observer to witness Mrs. V's seemingly unprovoked threats to mutilate her sons and her violent taping of
Randy's mouth. The boy presented a pale and trembling figure, his speech
—when he forgot her prohibitions and impulsively blurted out something
—was inarticulate and unintelligible. How often had his lips been sealed
before? How often had he cringed in fear, whimpering with less dignity
than his mother's dog? Mrs. V accurately described Randy's place in her
hierarchy of preference when, during this visit, she threatened to give
his dinner to her pets: "They deserve it more than you," she taunted, as
Randy's lips, already swollen from the taping, puckered yet again in sobs.

So much for Vicky's brothers. What of Vicky herself? With a sure
instinct for her own survival we have seen Vicky rapidly learning to
manipulate the system, to exploit weakness, and even to identify with the
aggressor if need be. Her mother many times contrasted her toughness
and spunk to her brothers' softness and cowardice. She frequently urged
her to hit them (before or after they hit her) and sought her collaboration
in punishing them, as in the last excerpt when Vicky gleefully cooperates
with her mother in taping Randy's mouth. Yet Vicky seems to be as much
a product of her mother's making as are her brothers. It may be that she,
too, as she grows older, will have the resilience knocked out of her,
although, at the age of three, this toughness seems to be her mainline to
survival as she negotiates the cross-currents of her mother's personality.

Vicky must adapt to the extreme environment in which she lives not
by developing conventionally approved intellectual and social skills but

first by learning to protect herself. Her necessary focus on survival skills may permanently stunt her growth in other areas or it may be only the foundation of a more complex pattern of adaptation in which "normal" achievements are reached later. We don't know. Our interest has been in tracing the effects of Vicky's human environment on her early development. What the longer term effects will be no one can say, although the figures of Vicky's two brothers imply one ominous possibility.

8

Terry:
A Double Bind

Terry is the subject of our final case study.* This little boy presents a sad and unique case. In him we witness the growth of a complex of emotional, social, and intellectual abnormalities. In his mother we see a woman trapped in the cage of her child's pathology and unable to find a way out either for herself or him. Terry's environment surely aggravates, if it does not produce, his abnormal development.

Our purpose in describing this case history is simple. We wish to show how the symptoms of a case such as Terry's (provisionally diagnosed as autism) present themselves in everyday life, how they develop in the course of early childhood, and how they may be accentuated by environmental factors. Our training is not in Clinical Psychology and no attempt will be made to relate this case to the clinical literature or to use specialized terms. Rather, we shall try to describe simply and straightforwardly what we saw as we observed this child, applying to his case methods that were designed for the study of normal children. Specifically, we shall try to show how Terry's experiences and environment differ from those of other children of similar age and circumstances whom we saw as developing excellently or relatively poorly—but normally. We hope that these data will be useful to clinicians who seldom have the chance to observe the development of abnormality *before* a child is admitted to therapy, or to view childhood pathology in the full context of a home and family.

*At the time of this writing Terry was thirty months old. We discontinued observing him and helped his mother get him admitted into therapy at a local medical center where he is still undergoing treatment as an out-patient.

TERRY'S INTELLECTUAL DEVELOPMENT

Terry was a year old when we started observing him. We learned about his family through the Boston Branch of the Maternal and Infant Health Project, his sister having been one of the subjects in that study. We applied our usual screening procedures for visual, auditory and physical handicaps to Terry and administered the Bayley Mental Development Index. Terry proved to be in good shape physically, and his mental development seemed above average (his Bayley Mental Development Index was 109). A preliminary interview with his mother also gave us no particular cause for concern except on one point: his mother reported that Terry had been an exceptionally good baby and had never cried until he was six months old. She was glad of this, since crying and fussing in her older children had irritated her greatly, and she found Terry a great relief. Otherwise, Terry's development according to his mother had been normal. He had viral pneumonia when he was about six months old, but few other infantile ailments.

It is important to note that, although Terry's performance on the Bayley at twelve months was above average, this was not the case for the other tests given at the same time. On our test of spatial abilities Terry ranked last in the group of twenty children his age in our study, and on our test of receptive language he tied for last place, obtaining a score of 0. Terry's performance on these tests, up until thirty months when we last tested him, continued to be exceptionally poor. Except for a slight improvement in performance on the spatial test at twenty-one months when he ranked sixteenth, Terry ranked last on every test given between fifteen and thirty months. At twenty-four months his Bayley Mental Development Index had plummeted from 109 to 66.

To put it more concretely, at two-and-a-half Terry's comprehension of language was what one would expect of a one-year-old child. He seemed to understand a few simple, familiar words and phrases like "hi," "bye," "book," "drink," "cookie," "get your baba," "give me the book," but showed no understanding (or at least he did not respond) of other instructions. Requests from his mother such as "throw the ball," or "turn off the TV," and directives from the examiner such as "write on the paper," or "put the keys in the cup," fell on deaf ears. Terry did not look toward the speaker or give any sign that he knew he was being spoken to. Of course, it is impossible to determine whether Terry was deliberately ignoring these adults or just did not understand their instructions. His mother's interpretation was that Terry "just doesn't give a damn," and his behavior certainly fit this description as well as any other.

At thirty months Terry's expressive language was also clearly abnormal. For the most part, it consisted of intonational babbling with a few intelligible words thrown in here and there. Terry sometimes repeated words used by an adult but often after a five or ten minute delay and in a random fashion. Interestingly, he was also able to count by rote up to twenty and to repeat the alphabet with a few prompts. He had learned this feat from *Sesame Street,* which he watched twice a day, every day. Of particular significance was his mother's report that Terry never addressed any one by name until he was nearly thirty months, when he started calling her "mama." Also he never asked for anything he wanted until he actually saw it. For example, long hours would pass without his having a meal, and Terry would show no sign of hunger until he heard the sounds of his mother preparing a meal in the kitchen. Then he would pound on the wall, kick, yell, and shriek, wanting to be instantly satisfied. Not surprisingly, his mother's attempts to toilet train him at about twenty-seven months totally failed. Terry still urinates and defecates at will on the linoleum of the living room, although he has understanding enough to remove his shorts before doing so.

SOCIO-EMOTIONAL DEVELOPMENT

Terry's social and emotional development has proceeded as poorly as his intellectual development. According to his mother, he was for a long time very unaffectionate to her and other members of the family, except for his nine-year-old brother, Kim, who acts as his "protector." Not until he was about twenty-seven months old did he show a liking for sitting on his mother's lap or cuddling or kissing. (Recall that a few months after he also first started calling her "mama.") But even now his mood often changes unpredictably and he will suddenly slap or kick his mother without provocation. To his father, his five-year-old sister, relatives, and visitors, he is alternately hostile or totally indifferent. He acts as if he were unaware of their presence except as restraining agents.

In his mother's eyes, the most difficult problems with Terry center on discipline, destructiveness, and attempts at escape. Terry doesn't listen to his mother at all. No matter how often she tells him not to do something, he continues to do it. He doesn't care how hard or how often he is punished. It just doesn't sink in. He acts as if he were deaf and insensitive to pain, showing little or no reaction to being yelled at, slapped, whipped, or locked in.

Terry's destructiveness has increased steadily from the age of one. He regularly turns out the bureau drawers and kitchen cabinets (on the rare occasion he is allowed in the kitchen), tears down blinds, overturns lamps, peels off the wallpaper. The situation has become so intolerable that relatives now refuse to baby-sit. One nephew gave up in despair when Terry, age twenty-nine months, got out of his crib one night and "totally wrecked" the house, smashing china, tearing down curtains, breaking furniture, and ripping the bedclothes.

More recent phenomena are Terry's attempts to escape from the house. A few months after his second birthday he got out of the house in the snow and took off all his clothes. It was freezing cold but he seemed to feel no discomfort. At thirty months he climbed out of the window of his bedroom (although he is allegedly terrified of heights) and was found wandering about up the street in a daze.

Without judging whether Terry's environment has caused his imperviousness to discipline, his destructiveness, and attempts to escape, let us simply record some abnormal aspects of Terry's daily routine. First note that he spends almost his entire day confined to a playpen (used constantly until he was eighteen months old), or to one rather bare room of the house. All doors to this—the living room—are usually locked, and the one open exit to the kitchen is more often than not barred with a gate or blocked with a toy chest. Only three times in fifteen separate one-hour visits to his home did we see Terry in any room other than the living room, and never did we see him outside the house.

Our observations are entirely consistent with his mother's frank acknowledgement that she seldom allows him out of the living room and almost never takes him outdoors, this being too much of a trial. She hates to cross the street in front of the house with him, since he refuses to hold her hand and darts into the traffic. Taking him to the beach or the park for an outing is equally nerve-wracking. As likely as not, he will end up climbing into car windows, throwing things at people, running off to hide, and so on. His mother cannot even leave him to play alone on the front porch, for he immediately kicks in the railings and is off into the street.

In brief, Terry spends almost all his waking hours confined to one room of the house and his mother spends nearly all of her time at home making sure he stays in. She goes out of the house no more than one night or so per week. She seldom goes shopping or visiting friends. She, like her son, is caged in.

TERRY'S HUMAN AND PHYSICAL ENVIRONMENT

Before presenting our actual observations on Terry and his mother, a few words must be said about their social-class background and Terry's human and physical environment. Terry's family is working-class: his father works as a truck driver, earns between $7,000 and $12,000 per year, and has a high school education. His mother never finished high school and has not worked outside the house since she married. Both parents are Irish Catholic. Terry has a brother six years older and a sister three years older. The family lives in a seven-room apartment in a fairly well maintained two-family house in an Irish section of Boston. Furnishings in the apartment are drab and worn, but Mrs. T keeps the apartment clean and neat, despite Terry's maraudings.

For Terry, the home essentially consists of the living room to which he is confined for almost all his waking hours. Its main furnishings—an old sofa, armchair, side tables, a toy chest—are nondescript to an outsider who does not have to look at them twelve hours a day. A visitor to Terry's home may remember only one outstanding feature of the living room—a large television set. Television is Terry's main source of intellectual and social stimulation. He sits for hours rocking before it, like a housewife addicted to soap operas. Sometimes as another television in the kitchen blares forth the same commercial as the one in the living room, Terry runs from one set to another, alternately baffled and excited at this electronic magic.

We must suppose that among Terry's main friends are the Muppets of *Sesame Street* who taught him his numbers and letters, Lucy of the *Lucy Show,* and the shifting band of two-dimensional people who inhabit the quiz shows and soap operas of television land. Real people do not often interact with Terry. His mother is at home all day but stays away from him as much as possible, except to restrain him. Occasionally his older brother or his sister plays with him briefly, but we never saw his father pay attention to Terry, nor did he ever seem to seek his notice.

Thus, Terry is a child who has to rely almost completely on his own limited resources for his development. Much of his time is spent watching television. Much is devoted to repetitive and rather primitive play with the fair number of toys his mother has bought him. On the positive side we should note that some of Terry's solitary play with toys and household objects is sustained, systematic, inventive, and intellectually productive. His chief lack is not of exploration of the physical environment (even though this is very often restricted by his mother) but of interaction with other people and the stimulation of live language. It is possible that this isolation from other people and consequent inability to relate to them is the chief factor in Terry's poor test performance, a prerequisite of every test being the child's willingness to take directives from an adult. We are struck by the fact that during our observations Terry often tried to master the use of fine-motor materials and occasionally seemed fascinated by some physical phenomenon, yet his test scores showed little improvement in these areas as he matured. In the test session his main intent was to destroy the test materials, and his reaction to adult directives was indifference or lack of comprehension.

Terry: Excerpt 1

Terry, a year old, is standing in his playpen before the television set in the living room. His sister, Hilary, is sitting on the couch and both children are watching *Sesame Street*. Their mother is busy in the kitchen.

> Terry watches **Sesame Street** on TV. (A counting sequence followed by scenes of a boy at a playground.)
> Terry continues watching. (Sequence of beavers in their homes over water.) Terry rocks from one foot to the other as he watches.
> Terry continues watching. (Sequence of a boy building a home for people with four walls; concept of different types of homes for differnt animals, including men.) Terry rocks back and forth as he watches.
> Terry watches TV. (Continuing sequence.)
> Terry watches TV. (Number "7" being presented.)
> Terry watches TV. (Puppets enact comic story about "7.")
> Terry watches TV. Terry looks at his sister, Hilary, sitting on the couch and drinking from a glass. He watches the counting on the TV. He looks at his sister drinking.
> Terry rocks from one foot to another, watching the TV. (Counting sequence.)
> Terry sits in his playpen and watches TV. (Counting sequence.) He touches and looks at a crib toy, then looks at a ring which is partially hidden because it has fallen part-way down a crack in the playpen. Terry pulls at it and it comes out of the crack.
> Terry holds the ring and chews on the strap of the crib toy to which it is attached. Terry looks at the TV. (Counting sequence.) He crawls closer to the TV. Terry stands and rocks watching **Sesame Street.**

Commentary. It is always risky to make too much of an initial observation. The observer is a stranger to the mother and child, and consequently their behavior may not be typical. However, it is most unusual in our experience for a mother to spend no time interacting with a child in our first visit to the home. Normally, the mother overinteracts to impress the observer and even siblings are usually congenial. But this first observation on Terry augurs things to come. Mother stays clear of him, sister sits close by but says not a word, and Terry sits mesmerized by *Sesame Street*, giving no clue of what, if anything, he is learning.

During our several visits Terry merely watched television most of the time we were observing him and in no case did anyone try to help him make sense of the program. Although we shall not provide any further excerpts of Terry's television viewing, per se, it must be remembered that this is a highly significant part of Terry's daily experience; indeed, according to his mother, Terry spends most of the day "glued to the TV."

Terry's dependence on television would not be so pathetic if he seemed to understand what was going on in the program he so avidly watched. After all, many other children in our study spent large amounts of time watching television, with apparent understanding. But in Terry's case, the medium seems not a message but a massage, softening his brain and tranquilizing his active body. Hundreds of hours of *Sesame Street* taught him the ABC's, two years of living with his brother and sister failed to teach him their names.

Terry: Excerpt 2

In this second observation made when Terry was nearly thirteen months old, we find him once again in the playpen in the living room. His sister is nearby watching *Sesame Street,* and his mother is sitting opposite him in the armchair reading the newspaper.

> Terry sits in the playpen in the living room. His sister, Hilary, comes in with an armful of toys and puts into the playpen a ball, two fire ladders, and other toys, as Terry looks on. Hilary leaves. Terry lies on his stomach and mouths a spoon. Hilary comes in and drops more toys in the playpen, including two small wooden dolls. Terry picks up a small doll and bangs it on the playpen floor (made of boards).
>
> Terry gets up then sits down again. He picks up a spoon and a toy chicken. Terry throws the chicken out of the playpen onto the living room floor and watches it fall. Terry mouths the spoon and babbles to Mother. Mother: "I see you," and smiles at him. Terry starts hiccuping. Mother: "You got the hiccups, uh?" Mother reads the newspaper. Terry mouths the spoon and looks at Hilary sitting on the couch. He puts the spoon at the back of his head and moves it up and down on his hair at his neck.
>
> Terry mouths the spoon and glances at the TV. He then brushes the doll on the playpen floor with the spoon. He drops the spoon and it falls between two boards of the playpen floor. Terry takes it out and tries to fit it in again without success. He tries again and again.
>
> Terry looks closely at the spoon then puts it in his mouth. He bends down to pick up a small wooden doll and the toy chicken and throws them out onto the floor. Mother: "Uh—now you haven't got them." Terry looks at Mother and claps his hands. Mother claps hers and smiles and calls, "Terry." Terry babbles and chortles with delight.

Commentary.   Terry's behavior in this observation seems in no way abnormal for a child of his age. He is interested in throwing objects and seeing them fall, he likes to mouth and manipulate small items, he tries to fit one thing into another, he studies the behavior of people around him. His mother's interaction with him is also normal and pleasant. She gives him security by sitting close by, she talks to him from time to time helping him to interpret events important in his world ("You got the hiccups, huh?" or "Now you haven't got them," when Terry throws the wooden dolls out of the playpen), and she plays little social games with him, clapping hands and smiling. His mother's interactions with Terry are brief and not very imaginative, but they are by no means atypical for a one-year-old's mother who has a limited education and no particular interest in the teaching of young children. It is not until later, when Terry is over eighteen months and is able to flex his muscles, so to speak, that his mother's interactions with him become harsh, restrictive, and punitive. This observation, then, should be remembered for its benign and normal qualities. We shall not observe any more experiences like this after Terry graduates from his playpen and intrudes into the domain of the living room and kitchen.

Terry: Excerpt 3

Terry was nearly fourteen months when this observation was made. We come upon him once again in his playpen in the living room. His mother and sister are also in the living room watching a television soap opera.

> Terry drinks from his bottle, standing in the playpen while watching a soap opera on TV. He throws down the bottle and picks up a wooden figure that fits into a Fisher-Price bus. Terry studies the figure, tries to put it in a hole in the bus, but fails. Terry puts his finger in the hole then pulls on the dial of a toy phone. At her mother's suggestion, Hilary puts one of the wooden figures that has fallen on the floor into the playpen for Terry and he picks it up.
>
> Terry tosses the figure onto the floor and watches it roll. He puts his finger into a hole of the bus. Hilary: "Hey, don't throw the people out." She retrieves the toys and repeats, "Don't throw the people out." Terry looks at the bus, turns it over, and looks at the bottom. He turns it right side up, rotates it slowly, studying it. He looks at Mother who waves: "Hi, Terry." Terry responds, "Hi." Terry turns the bus upside down and looks at the bottom, rotating it slowly and studying it.
>
> Hilary watches Terry. Terry babbles. Terry rotates the bus again, turning it over and over, babbling as he does so. Mother watches as Terry continues to rotate the bus. Terry chews on the bus a little and Mother watches him. Terry rotates the bus, chews on it, and studies it. Mother is now watching TV. Terry scratches the bus with his fingernail and touches the wheels.
>
> Terry picks up one of the wooden figures, puts it into a hole of the bus, then takes it out again. Terry sets another one in, then rubs his eyes. Terry pulls the toy telephone over by the cord. He dials the phone, picks up the receiver and says, "Lo, lo." Terry reaches into the bus, picks up a wooden figure and puts it into the bus.
>
> Terry drinks from his bottle. He picks up a wooden figure and tries to put it into the bus. Terry tosses down the figure and pushes the nipple of the bottle against the bus. Terry drinks from his bottle and watches a TV soap opera. He dials the toy phone, moving the dial back and forth, watching it move. Terry picks up the bus, looks at the bottom, then rotates it slowly, watching it from different angles.
>
> Terry watches Mother who's holding Hilary. He rotates the bus again,

watches TV, looks at Mother, drinks from his bottle, watches Mother, looks at the observer, then picks up a wooden figure and throws it on the floor.

Terry looks on the floor of his playpen. He tosses out one of the wooden figures, watching its trajectory. Terry watches Mother as he drinks from his bottle. Mother: "I see you, Terry." Terry: "Ha." Terry drinks from his bottle, leaning against the playpen and rocking. Terry looks at Mother. Mother: "Peek-a-boo," and peeps out first from one then from the other side of Hilary, who is sitting on her lap. Terry watches the TV and drinks from his bottle. He steps on his toy fire engine, jumps on it, then watches TV and drinks from his bottle at the same time.

Terry drinks from his bottle, babbling occasionally. He watches TV. Mother covers her face with her hands then removes her hands: "I see you, I see you." Terry laughs. Mother: "Peek-a-boo." Terry turns to the TV. He drinks from his bottle and watches TV. Mother whistles for Terry's attention. Terry watches TV. Mother watches Terry and smiles at him. Terry steps over the fire engine to turn to Mother. Mother claps for him.

Terry crawls on the floor of his playpen and puts his fingers down into the holes of the wooden bus. He tries to put one of the figures into the bus, fails, and pulls it out. Terry now tries to push the toy through the sides of the bus. He turns the bus upside down and looks in through the slats on the side. He pulls out the toy figure. He sets the figure into the bottom of the bus. He rights the bus and puts a figure in, trying to fit the toy into the hole. He takes it out again and sets it on top of the hole.

Terry moves around, babbling to himself. He looks at TV, then at his sister. He tries to put a toy figure through the side of the bus, fails, puts the figure in through the top of the bus, then through the side. Terry drops the bus, hits the figure with the bus, hits the bus on the floor of his playpen, and laughs.

Commentary. This observation is remarkable for the persistent and systematic manner in which Terry concentrates on the task of understanding spatial relations. Terry studies the little bus, rotating it to see it from all sides. He comes back again and again to the problem of fitting the little wooden figure in the bus until he finally masters it. He even invents the new game of putting the figure in through the side of the bus instead of the top—obviously enjoying his experiment.

His mother's and sister's appreciation of his scientific feats is limited. His sister is irritated by his fascination with throwing objects to watch them fall and his mother breaks up his concentration by distracting him with social games already familiar to him. (Recall the social games of excerpt 2.) But for the most part, Mother and Hilary merely watch Terry and let him get on with his little projects that seem intellectually productive for a child of his age.

Terry's interest in toys designed for developing fine motor and spatial skills and in exploring and experimenting with his physical environment continues as a theme throughout our observations. However, as he grows older, a new element is introduced. His previously fairly neutral human environment becomes much more restrictive and punitive, as each observation becomes a contest of wills between Terry and his mother over his getting into things. The fairly warm, if limited, relationship that Terry had with his mother when he was confined to his playpen and could do little damage has vanished. Instead we see a mother who seems no longer to like her little son very much, and a little boy who regards his mother primarily as an agent of restraint.

Terry: Excerpt 4

This observation was made when Terry was a little over eighteen months old and had graduated from playpen to living room, with all exits barred.

> Terry sits in front of the bookshelf, pulling books out. He pulls out a book and picks up a piece of paper (his sister's school work-sheet) and looks at it. Terry pulls out another book. Mother comes over and says, "Terry no," and removes him saying, "Don't touch again," and slaps his hand. Terry babbles something back.
>
> Terry goes back and touches the books. Mother: "No!" Terry throws himself on the floor and whines. He gets up and picks up a doll and throws it on the floor. He throws it again. He gets up and marches over to look for the doll under the side table. His sister, Hilary, looks on and laughs. Terry gets up and laughs back. He babbles something and picks up a plastic bucket and throws it down on the floor. He marches back to the shelf and pulls at the books again.
>
> Mother yells "no" and goes to remove him. Terry whines and goes to a toy garage set on the floor, then walks to Hilary and Mother. Terry hugs his sister and she laughs. He sits down near Mother who is fixing his sister's hair. Mother pushes his head away roughly: "Get out of here. Go away." Terry laughs. He crawls to the garage set, fingers the elevator part, and pulls the stop sign in it.
>
> Terry touches and looks at the underside of the garage, then stands up and goes up to the shelf and pulls down a picture in a frame. Mother: "No," and goes to stop him. Terry babbles something and walks to look out the glass door (outer front door) and bangs on the glass panel. Mother: "Boo, come here." Terry ignores, pushes the door, and looks out at the street.
>
> Terry marches around then goes to pick up another framed picture. Mother: "Terry!" and comes to remove him. "Don't touch." Terry just laughs. Mother: "I am not playing with you." He goes and picks up another picture. Mother tells Hilary to get it from him and she does so. Terry tries to get it back. Mother goes to pull him away from the shelf. Mother: "Don't touch it again, you know it. Don't laugh, fresh kid." Terry laughs and walks to the TV.

Commentary.   The contrast in Terry's mother's behavior in this observation when Terry is no longer confined to his playpen and the previous observations is striking. *All* of her interactions with him now take the form of restriction. No more social games, no more snippets of conversation, mostly an unrelieved barrage of "no's" and slaps on the hand when Terry resists. Terry does not accept this treatment passively. He whines, throws himself on the floor, bangs on furniture in anger, laughs at his mother, and continues disobeying her.

Of course, almost every mother has her bad days when a child's getting into things gets on her nerves and patience goes out the window. Unfortunately, Terry's interaction with his mother in this excerpt has become the rule rather than the exception, as the next excerpt confirms.

Terry: Excerpt 5
Two weeks later we find Terry for the first time wandering about in the kitchen.

> Terry wanders about, eating a cookie. He toddles to the window and taps the screen. He walks through the kitchen still eating the cookie. Terry starts to walk behind the stove. Mother sees him and calls, "No, Terry!" She takes him by the hand and leads him out.
>
> Terry returns to the stove. Mother shouts, "No!", takes him by the hand, and pulls him out from behind the stove. Terry reaches into the garbage. Mother moves his hands. (Sequence is repeated three times.) Mother finally says, "I'm not playing," and slaps his hands. Terry walks away, touching the drawer handle as he goes past. Terry eats his cookie and wanders about. He walks to the back door, rubs his hands across the door, then touches the door knob.
>
> Terry walks to the center of the room, touching chairs as he walks past them. Terry wanders about, touches the blender and the feeding table as he goes past. Terry walks around in the kitchen, then briefly watches Mother folding laundry in the next room. Terry toddles through the kitchen, goes over to the garbage can and touches the garbage. Mother comes into the kitchen and slaps his hands. Terry immediately goes to the garbage again. Mother spanks his bottom and Terry shrieks.
>
> Terry walks to the garbage, shrieking. Mother slaps his hands. Terry cries. He walks to Mother and then follows her into the bedroom. Mother: "Come on."

Commentary.   We hardly need comment further on this observation. It seems but a replay of the previous excerpt, a little more poignant perhaps because the kitchen is essentially unexplored territory for Terry and his urge to touch more irresistible. Obviously, a mother is justified in preventing a child from breaking kitchen appliances or rummaging in the garbage, but a skillful one soon finds ways of channeling her child's curiosity towards pots and pans, cans of food, or water in the sink— materials that will keep a one-year-old busy, happy, and safe for a long time while she does her chores. It is remarkable that in fifteen one-hour observations we almost never saw Terry being allowed to play with a household object for any length of time without some form of restriction being imposed. One predictable consequence of this unrelieved restriction is that Terry's curiosity about his physical environment will become increasingly shallow and insatiable. Typically, we shall see him wandering from object to object, touching, poking, pulling, throwing and yanking things. This disorderly behavior will quickly exasperate his mother who then applies restrictions, and the vicious cycle repeats itself. An observation on Terry made three months later when he had just turned two is a case in point.

Terry: Excerpt 6

The scene opens with Terry, age twenty-five months, in the kitchen eating lunch with his mother, Hilary, his mother's friend, and the friends' daughter, Margaret.

> Terry babbles to himself. Mother: "Hey, Terry!" He looks at Mother as she pours milk into her tea. Terry babbles something. Mother: "Oh yeah? 1, 2, 3." He babbles some more and Mother listens. Margaret says to Terry, "One." Terry continues, "Two, three," Margaret says, "Four, five." Terry: "Nine, ten." Everyone laughs. Margaret claps her hands (praising Terry). Margaret says again, "One, one, one." Terry ignores her. Margaret repeats, "One." Terry ignores her. Mother looks disappointed or perhaps angry. Terry climbs down from the chair to the floor.
>
> Margaret says to him, "Want to sit on my lap?" Terry ignores her and walks away and goes behind Mother to climb on another chair by the stove. Mother goes and closes the cabinet above the chair, saying, "No!" Terry goes back to the kitchen table with Mother, who pats his head. Terry goes to the ice box, then turns the doorknob on the door next to it. Mother: "No!" Terry tries to open the door again. Mother: "No!" Margaret gets up to close the door as Terry gets it open. Terry says, "See," and babbles something as he tries to open the door again. Mother: "No!" Terry ignores Mother and continues trying to open the door. Mother: "Terry, no!" (Sharply.)
>
> Terry complies, then says, "Bye, bye," and goes to pull on the kitchen window. Mother looks on. Terry looks out onto the driveway. He goes to the other side of the refrigerator and tries to reach up for a sheet of art work hanging on a door. He walks back to the chair next to the stove. Mother: "No! Get down," as he tries to climb up on it. Mother pulls him away. Terry goes to the kitchen table as Mother looks on. He picks up a sandwich, eats, and walks out to his brother's room next to the kitchen.
>
> Terry walks to a door leading to another room and opens and shuts the door repeatedly. Mother comes in: "Oh, no!" Mother blocks him and fastens the hook on the door so it stays shut. Terry goes to pick up a toy hammer off the floor, shakes it and bangs it on the wall then takes it to the kitchen. He goes to the door next to the refrigerator again and bangs the hammer on the door.
>
> Mother: "No! No!" Terry bangs on the cabinet nearby and babbles to himself. He picks up his sandwich and takes a bite. He goes to the dryer and tries to open the door by pulling the handle without success. Terry then goes to the serving cart and touches a small doll on it. Terry babbles to himself, walks to the cart, and tries to lift the top open. Terry comes around the clothes rack and goes to the door that his mother had just fastened.
>
> Terry turns the doorknob, trying to open it. He goes to a chest of drawers

and pulls a folded-up stool out and puts it on the floor and pulls a metal box (1-½ inches long by 1 inch wide) out of the dresser. He puts it flat on the floor. Mother comes in: "No, no!" Mother takes the box away to the kitchen.

Commentary. A few weeks before this observation was made Terry was tested with the Bayley Mental Development Index and with tests of receptive language and spatial abilities in his mother's presence. Mrs. T is now well aware that Terry's development is not quite normal. His failure to respond to instructions from the examiner and his attempts to destroy the test materials have direct counterparts in his everyday behavior at home, and she is beginning to wonder whether he really understands what she says or whether he was just "born bad."

By age two Terry is giving so little indication to his mother that he is learning from his explorations of household objects that her inclination to preserve her possessions by restricting his exploration seems justified. Her view is that all he wants to do is to break and destroy things and Terry does indeed act that way. Similarly, Terry's language development has progressed so poorly that his mother seems to try less and less to teach him, even while becoming increasingly anxious that he will never learn to talk. Her disappointment with Terry's failure to perform for a visitor in the last excerpt is plain, but she makes no attempt to coax him to count (probably, she felt she would not succeed anyway) and says not another word to him by way of conversation. Recall that when Terry was twelve to fifteen months old Mrs. T would occasionally indulge in pleasant chitchat of the "how're you doing" variety and from time to time would comment on events for his benefit. (See excerpts 2 and 3.) But she now seldom makes even this limited effort and most of her remarks signal restriction. Terry meanwhile has become less and less responsive to social stimulation and has learned to tune out other people. His refusal to continue the counting game is an exact counterpart to his refusal to play the games of test-taking.

We shall end our observations on Terry with one more excerpt that, as eloquently as any, shows Terry's deteriorating ability to relate to other people.

Terry: Excerpt 7

The setting for this observation is again the living room. A gate bars the exit to the kitchen and Terry, age twenty-seven months, is confined to the living room and a small adjacent bedroom, the door of which is closed. Terry's brother, Kim, and his sister, Hilary, are in the living room while his mother is busy in the kitchen.

Terry is sitting on a coffee table, looking at a quiz show on television. Kim says to Terry, "How about a game of hockey?" Kim is swatting at a small ball with a plastic hockey stick. Terry does not respond but simply stares at his brother. Suddenly Terry gets off the table and walks around and around in a circle. His brother and sister are swatting the ball back and forth, and he is in their field but not interacting with them.

Kim swats the ball and mistakenly looks for it under a couch. Terry runs to a corner of the room to find the ball (it had, in fact, rolled there) and picks it up. Terry tries to keep the ball for himself, but Kim takes it away. Terry stands before the television looking at the quiz show. Suddenly he starts running back and forth from one end of the room to the other, each time placing his palms on the wall and gently banging his head against it. He looks up at Hilary who is changing the channel on the TV.

Terry looks at **The Newlywed Game** on television. Kim and Hilary continue to play catch, shouting playfully at each other. Suddenly, Terry runs around in a circle in the middle of the room, five or six times, again interfering with the game, but not interacting with his brother and sister.

Terry collapses on the floor on his tummy, head down. He abruptly sits up and looks at TV. Kim and Hilary continue to play with the ball, throwing it hard across the room. Terry looks at the TV, showing no interest in their game.

Terry continues to look at the TV, standing close to the television set, while Kim and Hilary continue their noisy game.

Terry looks at the TV. He suddenly jumps up and follows Kim, then just as suddenly sits down on the floor and looks at the television program. Terry jumps and runs after Hilary, then circles back, sits on the floor and looks at TV. Again, he abruptly gets up, circles in the middle of the room, then suddenly sits down and looks at the TV. Terry repeats this pattern twice while his brother and sister ignore him and continue with their game.

Terry looks at the TV. He suddenly runs to the toy chest against the wall and climbs up on it. Mother calls out to his brother from the kitchen. Terry picks up a small button from the toy chest and returns to the TV. He looks at the TV, fingering the button.

Kim and Hilary squabble over the ball. Terry gazes at the TV, paying no attention to their fight. Terry pulls a coffee table over to the TV and climbs up on it.

Terry looks at the TV while standing on the table. He climbs up and down the table. His sister comes over and tries to pull the table away from in front of the TV. (Either he is barring her view or the table is in the way of the game.) Terry shrieks in anger, pulling the table back from her.

Mother calls from the kitchen: "Terry!" (Scolding him.) Terry runs to the gate barring the exit to the kitchen and hangs on it, looking in his mother's direction. Kim and Hilary squabble over their ball. Terry picks up a small truck and pushes it along on the floor. Kim and Hilary fight over the ball, but Terry pays no attention. Mother shouts from the kitchen: "Kim, come here!" Terry runs to the gate (as if she had called **him)** and says, "Okay." Terry hangs on the gate looking toward Mother in the hall. Mother deliberately ignores him, as she waits for Kim to come.

Commentary. Terry's behavior in this excerpt is nervous, random, and bizarre. It is as if the social pressure and the confinement to a small room with two other active, noisy, squabbling children has shattered his equilibrium. Our transcript of this observation falls far short of capturing its tragic and traumatic quality, but Terry's behavior—his ritualistic circling, his head banging, his staring into space—was so extreme that the observer felt sure that this young child was close to breaking point. It was this observation more than any other that convinced us that Terry needed treatment.

Our observations on Terry are now ended. We have witnessed in these pages the growth in a very young child of a complex of emotional, social, and intellectual abnormalities. We have not tried to diagnose Terry's difficulties; it is not within our competence to do so. Our purpose in presenting this case study is quite a different one. It is to describe simply and straightforwardly what we saw as we observed this child, using methods of study designed for normal children.

When we began our study of Terry at the age of one, we did not suspect that he would develop atypically. Initial physical and mental tests did not clearly distinguish him from other children in our sample, and his mother's account of Terry's infancy revealed nothing particularly alarming. What, then, is so different about Terry's development? First is his striking lack of language, either receptive or expressive. His test performance, as early as the age of one, consistently placed him at the bottom of our sample, and he seemed to make little improvement from test to test. At thirty months his language skills were still at the level of a twelve- to fifteen-month-old child. Our observations on Terry are entirely consistent with his test performance. Reviewing our transcripts we find that Terry occasionally babbled but seldom talked intelligibly, his speech being limited to words like "okay," "bye-bye," "lo-lo" (hello), and the parroting of numbers and letters heard on *Sesame Street*. Significantly, we can find no instance of his addressing anyone by name (not even "mama") or labeling an object or verbally expressing a need (not even for food or drink). There can be no doubt that Terry's speech development is greatly retarded, but this in itself does not make him intellectually abnormal. There are reports enough of geniuses who did not talk until they were past three.

A more reliable gauge of a young child's development is his *understanding* of language. However, in Terry's case there are obvious complicating factors. On tests of receptive language Terry performed poorly from the start, but the examiner could never be sure whether or not he understood what she said or whether he was simply unwilling to cooperate. Either interpretation is consistent with our observations, in which Terry usually ignored and disobeyed directives from his mother. Does he not understand what he is told? Not remember? Not care? We cannot be absolutely sure. What, also, of the large amount of time Terry spends watching television? Does he understand its language? What does he get out of it? Again, we have no incontrovertible evidence to help us decide either way.

Let us turn now to Terry's nonverbal abilities. Here, tests and observations are much less consistent. Terry's performance on tests of reasoning (essentially object permanence) and spatial abilities was very poor at twelve months and showed only slight improvement over the next eighteen months. But again his uncooperativeness with the tester makes it difficult to assess his performance. Every test, no matter how nonverbal, requires a child to accept directives from an adult, and ours are no exception. Observations of Terry's spontaneous behavior did include several instances of his engaging in systematic play with spatial and fine motor materials. As much as any other child, he seemed fascinated by physical phenomena and took time to study and experiment on such scientific topics as gravity, angles, trajectories, momentum, and cause and effect. We have no reason to suppose that Terry did not learn from this type of play but rather that he might not show what he knew on a test.

Terry's poor social development—his deteriorating ability to relate to other people—seems, therefore, to be the key to understanding his difficulties. In our initial observations of Terry we see a lovable and fairly outgoing little boy. He laughs when his mother plays peek-a-boo; he chortles with delight when they clap hands together; he cuddles up to his sister and touches her smiling face. In our final observations of Terry we see a child who is obstreperous, intractable, and impervious to discipline. He has withdrawn from social contact and is fast learning to tune out the overtures and demands of other people. A noisy game of catch between his brother and sister seems to shatter his equilibrium. What has happened to Terry in the interim?

Let us go back and analyze in more detail Terry's social experiences. Even between the ages of twelve to fifteen months he has a strikingly barren social life. He spends nearly all his waking hours in a playpen, being thus entirely dependent on other people to initiate social contact. These contacts do not occur very often. Terry's family interact with him only in brief snatches, and Terry himself makes only very rare attempts to gain their attention. He seldom seems to be trying to communicate with others. He never seems to use others as resources either for satisfying physical need or for stimulation. All his social interactions with his mother and siblings take the form of social games and exchanges of affection, all very brief and perfunctory.

Terry's social experiences after the age of eighteen months, when he has left his playpen for the living room and kitchen, become monotonously harsh. The occasional pleasant chit-chat and social games have nearly vanished from his life, and almost all of his mother's approaches to him take the form of restriction, threat, and punishment. It may be that unruly behavior is Terry's only way of gaining her attention, or he may be simply unable to understand what she wants of him. Whatever the reason, the relationship between this mother and child is striking in its one-dimensionality. Terry is the provocateur, mother the restraining agent. Terry touches, mother says "don't." Terry touches a second time, mother restrains him bodily. Terry touches a third time, mother slaps. This ritual repeated over and over again is both absurd and tragic. Child and mother seem caught in a trap in which both present extreme human environments for each other which neither can successfully adapt to or change.

We end this case history of Terry with the perennial question: Are Terry's abnormalities congenital or are they caused by his environment? Probably the answer will prove to be both. It seems to us that the value of Terry's story lies not in any possibility of weighing up constitutional and environmental contributions to Terry's condition, but in seeing how, over the course of time, an environment may work to help fulfill an inborn prophecy.

Epilogue

In this book we have described in concrete detail the everyday experiences of eight young children growing up in the natural environments of their homes. We have tried to show the complex relationship that exists between the intellectual development of the child and the social and cultural nexus in which he lives and grows. Our case studies depict an *active* child who is intrinsically motivated to play and behave in ways that promote his own development. Such a child fashions his own intellectually valuable experiences through his own intellectually competent behavior.

But the child's behavior does not occur in a vacuum. Enveloping him always is a human and physical environment that plays a number of direct and indirect roles in encouraging him to act intelligently and in providing him with experiences from which he can learn. Our interest in these roles played by the environment has led us to pay particular attention to the influence of the mother on the child. But the many detailed observations that we have provided speak equally well to the influence of the child on his mother and the effects of the child's behavior on himself. For us, the relationship between the child and his environment is never one way, although for purposes of exposition one direction of influence has been emphasized.

The child's intellectual development is also intimately connected with his social and emotional development, and we are keenly aware that our interpretation of the child's experiences primarily in terms of his intellectual development implies an arbitrary and artificial distinction. The child is an entity and so is his development. Many of the experiences that we have reported might equally well be analyzed in terms of the child's social and emotional development and the opportunity they provide for his social and emotional learning. This, in fact, is the next task to which we shall turn in our attempt to understand, through observation, reflection, and research, the meaning of childhood experiences.

Many years ago John Dewey remarked:

> Just as no man lives or dies to himself, so no experience lives or dies to itself. Wholly independent of desire or intent, every experience lives on in further experiences. Hence the central problem of an education based on experience is to select the kind of present experiences that live fruitfully and creatively in subsequent experience.*

The problem posed by Dewey continues to challenge us. It is to decide which experiences are truly educative—intellectually, socially and emotionally—and how those who care for children can help bring them about.

---

*J. Dewey, *Experience and Education* (New York: Collier, 1963 [originally written in 1938]), pp. 25-28.